MONTH-TO-MONTH RENTAL AGREEMENT FORMS BOOK

NAME	
EMAIL	
PHONE	
ADDRESS	

FORM INFORMATION

Start Date:	End Date:

All rights reserved. No part of this book may be reproduced in any form by any electronic or mechanical means including photocopying, recording, or information storage and retrieval without permission in writing from the author.

IF FOUND, PLEASE CONTACT OR

LIKE THIS FORM BOOK? PLEASE LEAVE A REVIEW ON AMAZON. THANKS!

MONTH-TO-MONTH RENTAL **AGREEMENT**

This lease agreement is made is made this ____________ by and (between/among) ______________ ______________ [Landlord] and ____________________, [and other Tenants,] collectively [Tenant]. Each Tenant is jointly and severally liable for the payment of rent to the landlord and performance of all other terms in this Agreement.

[PREMISES]

Landlord hereby leases the premises located at ______________________________ City of ______________, State of ______________________ [Premises] to Tenant.

[LEASE TERM]

The Lease will start on ___ of __________, 20___ and will continue as a month-to-month tenancy. To terminate tenancy, the Landlord or Tenant must give the other party a ______ day written notice of Lease non-renewal.

[LEASE PAYMENTS]

The Tenant agrees to pay Landlord for the use of the Premises in the amount of $ ______, payable in advance on the first day of each month, except when day falls on a legal holiday or weekend, in which case rent is due on the next business day. Rent will be paid to Landlord at Landlord's address provided herein (or to other places as directed by Landlord) by mail to ______________________________ _____ or in person, at ______________________________.

Landlord will accept check made payable to ______________________________ _or cashier's check made payable to ______________________________ __or payment by ______________________ to______________________

[LATE FEE]

Rent paid after the ______ day of each month will be considered as late; and if rent is not paid within ______ days of such due date, Tenant agrees to pay a late fee of ________ per day for every day that the rent is late.

[INSUFFICIENT FUNDS]

Tenant agrees to pay a charge of __________ for each check given by Tenant to Landlord that is returned to landlord for lack of sufficient funds.

[SECURITY DEPOSIT]

Upon execution of this Lease, Tenant shall deposit the sum of ____________ to be held by the Landlord as security deposit for reasonable repair of damages to, or cleaning of the Premises upon the expiration or termination of this Lease, or other notable damages.

d and occupied for no other purpose than as dwelling and
nt and the following named adults ______________
____
nd the following named children ______________
____
ning a written consent from the Landlord.
r the following utilities and or services ______________
____
ntenance and or repairs ______________
____
premises without priorly obtaining a written consent from

ENTER]

ses during the term of this Agreement, the Landlord has
cessary without facing any liability and the Landlord may

[AMENDMENTS]

The Landlord and Tenant agree that any amendments made to this Agreement must be in writing where they must be signed by both the Landlord and the Tenant. As such any amendment made by the parties will be applied to this Agreement.

[GOVERNING LAW]

This Agreement shall be governed by and construed in accordance with the laws of ______________ ______________________________

TENANT

Name ______________________
Signature ______________________
Date ______________________
Witness ______________________
Phone ______________________
Address ______________________
____
Signature ______________________
Date ______________________

LANDLORD

Name ______________________
Signature ______________________
Date ______________________
Address ______________________
____
Witness ______________________
Phone ______________________
Address ______________________
Signature____________Date______

MONTH-TO-MONTH RENTAL **AGREEMENT**

This lease agreement is made this __________ by and (between/among) _______ ___ ___ ___ ___ ___ ___ [Landlord] and ___ ___ ___ ___ ___ ___, [and other Tenants,] collectively [Tenant]. Each Tenant is jointly and severally liable for the payment of rent to the landlord and performance of all other terms in this Agreement.

[PREMISES]

Landlord hereby leases the premises located at ___ ___ ___ ___ ___ ___ ___ ___ ___ ___ City of ___ ___ ___ ___ ___, State of ___ ___ ___ ___ ___ ___ ___ ___ [Premises] to Tenant.

[LEASE TERM]

The Lease will start on ___ of ___ ___ ___, 20 ___ and will continue as a month-to-month tenancy. To terminate tenancy, the Landlord or Tenant must give the other party a ___ ___ day written notice of lease non-renewal.

[LEASE PAYMENTS]

The Tenant agrees to pay Landlord for the use of the Premises in the amount of $ ___ __, payable in advance on the first day of each month, except when day falls on a legal holiday or weekend, in which case rent is due on the next business day. Rent will be paid to Landlord at Landlord's address provided herein (or to other places as directed by Landlord) by mail to ___ ___ ___ ___ ___ ___ ___ ___ ___ _ __ ___ or in person, at ___ ___ ___ ___ ___ ___ ___ ___ ___ ___ ___ ___ ___ __.
Landlord will accept check made payable to ______________________________
_or cashier's check made payable to ________________________________
__or payment by ___________________________ to_________________________

[LATE FEE]

Rent paid after the ___ ___ day of each month will be considered as late; and if rent is not paid within ___ ___ days of such due date, Tenant agrees to pay a late fee of ___ ___ ___ per day for every day that the rent is late.

[INSUFFICIENT FUNDS]

Tenant agrees to pay a charge of ___ ___ ___ for each check given by Tenant to Landlord that is returned to landlord for lack of sufficient funds.

[SECURITY DEPOSIT]

Upon execution of this Lease, Tenant shall deposit the sum of ____________to be held by the Landlord as security deposit for reasonable repair of damages to, or cleaning of the Premises upon the expiration or termination of this Lease, or other notable damages.

[USE OF PREMISES]

1. Tenant agrees that the Premises shall be used and occupied for no other purpose than as dwelling and that the Premises shall be occupied only by Tenant and the following named adults _____________

____

_____________________________ and the following named children _______________

____

__________ and no other without first obtaining a written consent from the Landlord.

2. The tenant hereby agrees to be responsible for the following utilities and or services ___ ___ ___ _

__ ___ ___ ___ ___ ___ ___ ___ ___ ___ ___ ___ ___ _________________

3. The Tenant is responsible for the following maintenance and or repairs ___ ___ ___ ___ ___ __

_ ___ ___ ___ ___ ___ ___ ___ ___ ___ ___ ___ ___ _____ ___ ___ ___ ___

4. The tenant agrees not to keep any pets on the premises without priorly obtaining a written consent from the Landlord.

[ABANDONMENT AND RIGHT TO ENTER]

In any case that the Tenant abandons the Premises during the term of this Agreement, the Landlord has the right to enter the Premises by any means necessary without facing any liability and the Landlord may terminate this Agreement.

[AMENDMENTS]

The Landlord and Tenant agree that any amendments made to this Agreement must be in writing where they must be signed by both the Landlord and the Tenant. As such any amendment made by the parties will be applied to this Agreement.

[GOVERNING LAW]

This Agreement shall be governed by and construed in accordance with the laws of ___ ___ ___ ___

___ ___ ___ ___ ___ ___ ___ ___ ___ ___ ___ ___ ___ ___ ___ _________________

TENANT

Name ___________________________

Signature _________________________

Date ____________________________

Witness __________________________

Phone ___________________________

Address __________________________

____

Signature ________________________

Date ___________________________

LANDLORD

Name ___________________________

Signature _________________________

Date ___________________________

Address __________________________

____

Witness __________________________

Phone ___________________________

Address __________________________

Signature____________Date___________

MONTH-TO-MONTH RENTAL **AGREEMENT**

This lease agreement is made this __________ by and (between/among) _______ ___ ___ ___

___ ___ ___ [Landlord] and ___ ___ ___ ___ ___ ___, [and other Tenants,] collectively [Tenant]. Each Tenant is jointly and severally liable for the payment of rent to the landlord and performance of all other terms in this Agreement.

[PREMISES]

Landlord hereby leases the premises located at ___ ___ ___ ___ ___ ___ ___ ___ ___ ___

City of ___ ___ ___ ___ ___, State of ___ ___ ___ ___ ___ ___ ___ ___ [Premises] to Tenant.

[LEASE TERM]

The Lease will start on ___ of ___ ___ ___, 20 ___ and will continue as a month-to-month tenancy. To terminate tenancy, the Landlord or Tenant must give the other party a ___ ___ day written notice of lease non-renewal.

[LEASE PAYMENTS]

The Tenant agrees to pay Landlord for the use of the Premises in the amount of $ ___ __, payable in advance on the first day of each month, except when day falls on a legal holiday or weekend, in which case rent is due on the next business day. Rent will be paid to Landlord at Landlord's address provided herein (or to other places as directed by Landlord) by mail to ___ ___ ___ ___ ___ ___ ___ ___ ___ ___ _

__ ___ or in person, at ___ ___ ___ ___ ___ ___ ___ ___ ___ ___ ___ ___ ___ ___ __.

Landlord will accept check made payable to ___________________________________

_or cashier's check made payable to ______________________________________

__or payment by ___________________________ to_________________________

[LATE FEE]

Rent paid after the ___ ___ day of each month will be considered as late; and if rent is not paid within ___ ___ days of such due date, Tenant agrees to pay a late fee of ___ ___ ___ per day for every day that the rent is late.

[INSUFFICIENT FUNDS]

Tenant agrees to pay a charge of ___ ___ ___ for each check given by Tenant to Landlord that is returned to landlord for lack of sufficient funds.

[SECURITY DEPOSIT]

Upon execution of this Lease, Tenant shall deposit the sum of ____________to be held by the Landlord as security deposit for reasonable repair of damages to, or cleaning of the Premises upon the expiration or termination of this Lease, or other notable damages.

[USE OF PREMISES]

1. Tenant agrees that the Premises shall be used and occupied for no other purpose than as dwelling and that the Premises shall be occupied only by Tenant and the following named adults _____________

____

______________________________ and the following named children _______________

____

__________ and no other without first obtaining a written consent from the Landlord.

2. The tenant hereby agrees to be responsible for the following utilities and or services ___ ___ ___ _

__ ___ ___ ___ ___ ___ ___ ___ ___ ___ ___ ___ ___ ___ _________________

3. The Tenant is responsible for the following maintenance and or repairs ___ ___ ___ ___ ___ __

_ ___ ___ ___ ___ ___ ___ ___ ___ ___ ___ ___ ___ _____ ___ ___ ___

4. The tenant agrees not to keep any pets on the premises without priorly obtaining a written consent from the Landlord.

[ABANDONMENT AND RIGHT TO ENTER]

In any case that the Tenant abandons the Premises during the term of this Agreement, the Landlord has the right to enter the Premises by any means necessary without facing any liability and the Landlord may terminate this Agreement.

[AMENDMENTS]

The Landlord and Tenant agree that any amendments made to this Agreement must be in writing where they must be signed by both the Landlord and the Tenant. As such any amendment made by the parties will be applied to this Agreement.

[GOVERNING LAW]

This Agreement shall be governed by and construed in accordance with the laws of ___ ___ ___ ___

___ ___ ___ ___ ___ ___ ___ ___ ___ ___ ___ ___ ___ ___ ___________________

TENANT

Name ____________________________

Signature _________________________

Date _____________________________

Witness ___________________________

Phone ____________________________

Address ___________________________

____

Signature _________________________

Date ____________________________

LANDLORD

Name ___________________________

Signature ________________________

Date ___________________________

Address _________________________

____

Witness _________________________

Phone __________________________

Address _________________________

Signature____________Date__________

MONTH-TO-MONTH RENTAL AGREEMENT

This lease agreement is made this __________ by and (between/among) _______ ___ ___ ___ ___ ___ ___ [Landlord] and ___ ___ ___ ___ ___ ___, [and other Tenants,] collectively [Tenant]. Each Tenant is jointly and severally liable for the payment of rent to the landlord and performance of all other terms in this Agreement.

[PREMISES]

Landlord hereby leases the premises located at ___ ___ ___ ___ ___ ___ ___ ___ ___ ___ City of ___ ___ ___ ___ ___, State of ___ ___ ___ ___ ___ ___ ___ ___ [Premises] to Tenant.

[LEASE TERM]

The Lease will start on ___ of ___ ___ ___, 20 ___ and will continue as a month-to-month tenancy. To terminate tenancy, the Landlord or Tenant must give the other party a ___ ___ day written notice of lease non-renewal.

[LEASE PAYMENTS]

The Tenant agrees to pay Landlord for the use of the Premises in the amount of $ ___ __, payable in advance on the first day of each month, except when day falls on a legal holiday or weekend, in which case rent is due on the next business day. Rent will be paid to Landlord at Landlord's address provided herein (or to other places as directed by Landlord) by mail to ___ ___ ___ ___ ___ ___ ___ ___ ___ ___ __ ___ or in person, at ___ ___ ___ ___ ___ ___ ___ ___ ___ ___ ___ ___ ___ __.
Landlord will accept check made payable to ______________________________
_or cashier's check made payable to ______________________________
__or payment by ____________________________ to____________________________

[LATE FEE]

Rent paid after the ___ ___ day of each month will be considered as late; and if rent is not paid within ___ ___ days of such due date, Tenant agrees to pay a late fee of ___ ___ ___ per day for every day that the rent is late.

[INSUFFICIENT FUNDS]

Tenant agrees to pay a charge of ___ ___ ___ for each check given by Tenant to Landlord that is returned to landlord for lack of sufficient funds.

[SECURITY DEPOSIT]

Upon execution of this Lease, Tenant shall deposit the sum of ____________to be held by the Landlord as security deposit for reasonable repair of damages to, or cleaning of the Premises upon the expiration or termination of this Lease, or other notable damages.

[USE OF PREMISES]

1. Tenant agrees that the Premises shall be used and occupied for no other purpose than as dwelling and that the Premises shall be occupied only by Tenant and the following named adults ______________

____

__________________________________ and the following named children ________________

____

__________ and no other without first obtaining a written consent from the Landlord.

2. The tenant hereby agrees to be responsible for the following utilities and or services ___ ___ ___ _

__ ___ ___ ___ ___ ___ ___ ___ ___ ___ ___ ___ ___ ___ __________________

3. The Tenant is responsible for the following maintenance and or repairs ___ ___ ___ ___ ___ __

_ ___ ___ ___ ___ ___ ___ ___ ___ ___ ___ ___ ___ ____ ___ ___ ___

4. The tenant agrees not to keep any pets on the premises without priorly obtaining a written consent from the Landlord.

[ABANDONMENT AND RIGHT TO ENTER]

In any case that the Tenant abandons the Premises during the term of this Agreement, the Landlord has the right to enter the Premises by any means necessary without facing any liability and the Landlord may terminate this Agreement.

[AMENDMENTS]

The Landlord and Tenant agree that any amendments made to this Agreement must be in writing where they must be signed by both the Landlord and the Tenant. As such any amendment made by the parties will be applied to this Agreement.

[GOVERNING LAW]

This Agreement shall be governed by and construed in accordance with the laws of ___ ___ ___ ___

___ ___ ___ ___ ___ ___ ___ ___ ___ ___ ___ ___ ___ ___________________

TENANT

Name ______________________________

Signature ___________________________

Date _______________________________

Witness _____________________________

Phone ______________________________

Address _____________________________

____

Signature __________________________

Date ______________________________

LANDLORD

Name ____________________________

Signature _________________________

Date ____________________________

Address __________________________

____

Witness __________________________

Phone ___________________________

Address __________________________

Signature____________Date___________

MONTH-TO-MONTH RENTAL AGREEMENT

This lease agreement is made this __________ by and (between/among) _______ ___ ___ ___ ___ ___ ___ [Landlord] and ___ ___ ___ ___ ___ ___, [and other Tenants,] collectively [Tenant]. Each Tenant is jointly and severally liable for the payment of rent to the landlord and performance of all other terms in this Agreement.

[PREMISES]

Landlord hereby leases the premises located at ___ ___ ___ ___ ___ ___ ___ ___ ___ ___

City of ___ ___ ___ ___ ___, State of ___ ___ ___ ___ ___ ___ ___ ___ [Premises] to Tenant.

[LEASE TERM]

The Lease will start on ___ of ___ ___ ___, 20 ___ and will continue as a month-to-month tenancy. To terminate tenancy, the Landlord or Tenant must give the other party a ___ ___ day written notice of lease non-renewal.

[LEASE PAYMENTS]

The Tenant agrees to pay Landlord for the use of the Premises in the amount of $ ___ __, payable in advance on the first day of each month, except when day falls on a legal holiday or weekend, in which case rent is due on the next business day. Rent will be paid to Landlord at Landlord's address provided herein (or to other places as directed by Landlord) by mail to ___ ___ ___ ___ ___ ___ ___ ___ ___ ___ _ __ ___ or in person, at ___ ___ ___ ___ ___ ___ ___ ___ ___ ___ ___ ___ ___ ___ __.

Landlord will accept check made payable to ______________________________

_or cashier's check made payable to ______________________________

__or payment by ___________________________ to___________________________

[LATE FEE]

Rent paid after the ___ ___ day of each month will be considered as late; and if rent is not paid within ___ ___ days of such due date, Tenant agrees to pay a late fee of ___ ___ ___ per day for every day that the rent is late.

[INSUFFICIENT FUNDS]

Tenant agrees to pay a charge of ___ ___ ___ for each check given by Tenant to Landlord that is returned to landlord for lack of sufficient funds.

[SECURITY DEPOSIT]

Upon execution of this Lease, Tenant shall deposit the sum of _____________to be held by the Landlord as security deposit for reasonable repair of damages to, or cleaning of the Premises upon the expiration or termination of this Lease, or other notable damages.

[USE OF PREMISES]

1. Tenant agrees that the Premises shall be used and occupied for no other purpose than as dwelling and that the Premises shall be occupied only by Tenant and the following named adults _____________

____

______________________________ and the following named children ______________

____

__________ and no other without first obtaining a written consent from the Landlord.

2. The tenant hereby agrees to be responsible for the following utilities and or services ___ ___ ___ _

__ ___ ___ ___ ___ ___ ___ ___ ___ ___ ___ ___ ___ ___ _________________

3. The Tenant is responsible for the following maintenance and or repairs ___ ___ ___ ___ ___ __

_ ___ ___ ___ ___ ___ ___ ___ ___ ___ ___ ___ ___ ____ ___ ___ ___

4. The tenant agrees not to keep any pets on the premises without priorly obtaining a written consent from the Landlord.

[ABANDONMENT AND RIGHT TO ENTER]

In any case that the Tenant abandons the Premises during the term of this Agreement, the Landlord has the right to enter the Premises by any means necessary without facing any liability and the Landlord may terminate this Agreement.

[AMENDMENTS]

The Landlord and Tenant agree that any amendments made to this Agreement must be in writing where they must be signed by both the Landlord and the Tenant. As such any amendment made by the parties will be applied to this Agreement.

[GOVERNING LAW]

This Agreement shall be governed by and construed in accordance with the laws of ___ ___ ___ ___

___ ___ ___ ___ ___ ___ ___ ___ ___ ___ ___ ___ ___ ___________________

TENANT

Name ____________________________

Signature ________________________

Date _____________________________

Witness __________________________

Phone ___________________________

Address __________________________

____

Signature ________________________

Date ____________________________

LANDLORD

Name ___________________________

Signature ________________________

Date ________________________ _

Address _________________________

____

Witness _________________________

Phone ___________________________

Address _________________________

Signature___________Date___________

MONTH-TO-MONTH RENTAL AGREEMENT

This lease agreement is made this __________ by and (between/among) _______ ___ ___ ___ ___ ___ ___ [Landlord] and ___ ___ ___ ___ ___ ___, [and other Tenants,] collectively [Tenant]. Each Tenant is jointly and severally liable for the payment of rent to the landlord and performance of all other terms in this Agreement.

[PREMISES]

Landlord hereby leases the premises located at ___ ___ ___ ___ ___ ___ ___ ___ ___ ___ City of ___ ___ ___ ___ ___, State of ___ ___ ___ ___ ___ ___ ___ ___ [Premises] to Tenant.

[LEASE TERM]

The Lease will start on ___ of ___ ___ ___, 20 ___ and will continue as a month-to-month tenancy. To terminate tenancy, the Landlord or Tenant must give the other party a ___ ___ day written notice of lease non-renewal.

[LEASE PAYMENTS]

The Tenant agrees to pay Landlord for the use of the Premises in the amount of $ ___ __, payable in advance on the first day of each month, except when day falls on a legal holiday or weekend, in which case rent is due on the next business day. Rent will be paid to Landlord at Landlord's address provided herein (or to other places as directed by Landlord) by mail to ___ ___ ___ ___ ___ ___ ___ ___ ___ ___ _ __ ___or in person, at ___ ___ ___ ___ ___ ___ ___ ___ ___ ___ ___ ___ ___ ___ __.
Landlord will accept check made payable to ______________________________
_or cashier's check made payable to ____________________________________
__or payment by ___________________________ to_________________________

[LATE FEE]

Rent paid after the ___ ___ day of each month will be considered as late; and if rent is not paid within ___ ___ days of such due date, Tenant agrees to pay a late fee of ___ ___ ___ per day for every day that the rent is late.

[INSUFFICIENT FUNDS]

Tenant agrees to pay a charge of ___ ___ ___ for each check given by Tenant to Landlord that is returned to landlord for lack of sufficient funds.

[SECURITY DEPOSIT]

Upon execution of this Lease, Tenant shall deposit the sum of _____________to be held by the Landlord as security deposit for reasonable repair of damages to, or cleaning of the Premises upon the expiration or termination of this Lease, or other notable damages.

[USE OF PREMISES]

1. Tenant agrees that the Premises shall be used and occupied for no other purpose than as dwelling and that the Premises shall be occupied only by Tenant and the following named adults _____________

____

______________________________ and the following named children _______________

____

__________ and no other without first obtaining a written consent from the Landlord.

2. The tenant hereby agrees to be responsible for the following utilities and or services ___ ___ ___ _

__ ___ ___ ___ ___ ___ ___ ___ ___ ___ ___ ___ ___ _________________

3. The Tenant is responsible for the following maintenance and or repairs ___ ___ ___ ___ ___ __

_ ___ ___ ___ ___ ___ ___ ___ ___ ___ ___ ___ ___ _____ ___ ___ ___ ___

4. The tenant agrees not to keep any pets on the premises without priorly obtaining a written consent from the Landlord.

[ABANDONMENT AND RIGHT TO ENTER]

In any case that the Tenant abandons the Premises during the term of this Agreement, the Landlord has the right to enter the Premises by any means necessary without facing any liability and the Landlord may terminate this Agreement.

[AMENDMENTS]

The Landlord and Tenant agree that any amendments made to this Agreement must be in writing where they must be signed by both the Landlord and the Tenant. As such any amendment made by the parties will be applied to this Agreement.

[GOVERNING LAW]

This Agreement shall be governed by and construed in accordance with the laws of ___ ___ ___ ___

___ ___ ___ ___ ___ ___ ___ ___ ___ ___ ___ ___ ____________________

TENANT

Name ____________________________

Signature _________________________

Date _____________________________

Witness ___________________________

Phone ____________________________

Address ___________________________

____

Signature _________________________

Date _____________________________

LANDLORD

Name ___________________________

Signature ________________________

Date __________________________ _

Address _________________________

____

Witness _________________________

Phone __________________________

Address _________________________

Signature___________Date__________

MONTH-TO-MONTH RENTAL AGREEMENT

This lease agreement is made this __________ by and (between/among) _______ ___ ___ ___ ___ ___ ___ [Landlord] and ___ ___ ___ ___ ___ ___, [and other Tenants,] collectively [Tenant]. Each Tenant is jointly and severally liable for the payment of rent to the landlord and performance of all other terms in this Agreement.

[PREMISES]

Landlord hereby leases the premises located at ___ ___ ___ ___ ___ ___ ___ ___ ___ ___

City of ___ ___ ___ ___ ___, State of ___ ___ ___ ___ ___ ___ ___ ___ [Premises] to Tenant.

[LEASE TERM]

The Lease will start on ___ of ___ ___ ___, 20 ___ and will continue as a month-to-month tenancy. To terminate tenancy, the Landlord or Tenant must give the other party a ___ ___ day written notice of lease non-renewal.

[LEASE PAYMENTS]

The Tenant agrees to pay Landlord for the use of the Premises in the amount of $ ___ __, payable in advance on the first day of each month, except when day falls on a legal holiday or weekend, in which case rent is due on the next business day. Rent will be paid to Landlord at Landlord's address provided herein (or to other places as directed by Landlord) by mail to ___ ___ ___ ___ ___ ___ ___ ___ ___ ___ _ __ ___ or in person, at ___ ___ ___ ___ ___ ___ ___ ___ ___ ___ ___ ___ ___ __.

Landlord will accept check made payable to ______________________________

_or cashier's check made payable to __________________________________

__or payment by __________________________ to_________________________

[LATE FEE]

Rent paid after the ___ ___ day of each month will be considered as late; and if rent is not paid within ___ ___ days of such due date, Tenant agrees to pay a late fee of ___ ___ ___ per day for every day that the rent is late.

[INSUFFICIENT FUNDS]

Tenant agrees to pay a charge of ___ ___ ___ for each check given by Tenant to Landlord that is returned to landlord for lack of sufficient funds.

[SECURITY DEPOSIT]

Upon execution of this Lease, Tenant shall deposit the sum of _____________to be held by the Landlord as security deposit for reasonable repair of damages to, or cleaning of the Premises upon the expiration or termination of this Lease, or other notable damages.

[USE OF PREMISES]

1. Tenant agrees that the Premises shall be used and occupied for no other purpose than as dwelling and that the Premises shall be occupied only by Tenant and the following named adults ______________

____

____________________________ and the following named children ______________

____

__________ and no other without first obtaining a written consent from the Landlord.

2. The tenant hereby agrees to be responsible for the following utilities and or services ___ ___ ___ _

__ ___ ___ ___ ___ ___ ___ ___ ___ ___ ___ ___ ___ _________________

3. The Tenant is responsible for the following maintenance and or repairs ___ ___ ___ ___ ___ __

_ ___ ___ ___ ___ ___ ___ ___ ___ ___ ___ ___ ___ _____ ___ ___ ___

4. The tenant agrees not to keep any pets on the premises without priorly obtaining a written consent from the Landlord.

[ABANDONMENT AND RIGHT TO ENTER]

In any case that the Tenant abandons the Premises during the term of this Agreement, the Landlord has the right to enter the Premises by any means necessary without facing any liability and the Landlord may terminate this Agreement.

[AMENDMENTS]

The Landlord and Tenant agree that any amendments made to this Agreement must be in writing where they must be signed by both the Landlord and the Tenant. As such any amendment made by the parties will be applied to this Agreement.

[GOVERNING LAW]

This Agreement shall be governed by and construed in accordance with the laws of ___ ___ ___ ___

___ ___ ___ ___ ___ ___ ___ ___ ___ ___ ___ ___ _____________________

TENANT

Name ____________________________

Signature __________________________

Date _____________________________

Witness ___________________________

Phone ____________________________

Address ___________________________

____

Signature _________________________

Date ____________________________

LANDLORD

Name ___________________________

Signature ________________________

Date __________________________ _

Address _________________________

____

Witness _________________________

Phone ___________________________

Address _________________________

Signature___________Date__________

MONTH-TO-MONTH RENTAL AGREEMENT

This lease agreement is made this __________ by and (between/among) _______ ___ ___ ___ ___ ___ ___ [Landlord] and ___ ___ ___ ___ ___ ___ , [and other Tenants,] collectively [Tenant]. Each Tenant is jointly and severally liable for the payment of rent to the landlord and performance of all other terms in this Agreement.

[PREMISES]

Landlord hereby leases the premises located at ___ ___ ___ ___ ___ ___ ___ ___ ___ ___ City of ___ ___ ___ ___ ___, State of ___ ___ ___ ___ ___ ___ ___ ___ [Premises] to Tenant.

[LEASE TERM]

The Lease will start on ___ of ___ ___ ___, 20 ___ and will continue as a month-to-month tenancy. To terminate tenancy, the Landlord or Tenant must give the other party a ___ ___ day written notice of lease non-renewal.

[LEASE PAYMENTS]

The Tenant agrees to pay Landlord for the use of the Premises in the amount of $ ___ __, payable in advance on the first day of each month, except when day falls on a legal holiday or weekend, in which case rent is due on the next business day. Rent will be paid to Landlord at Landlord's address provided herein (or to other places as directed by Landlord) by mail to ___ ___ ___ ___ ___ ___ ___ ___ ___ ___ _ __ ___ or in person, at ___ ___ ___ ___ ___ ___ ___ ___ ___ ___ ___ ___ ___ ___ __.

Landlord will accept check made payable to ______________________________________ _or cashier's check made payable to ____ __or payment by ___________________________ to_________________________

[LATE FEE]

Rent paid after the ___ ___ day of each month will be considered as late; and if rent is not paid within ___ ___ days of such due date, Tenant agrees to pay a late fee of ___ ___ ___ per day for every day that the rent is late.

[INSUFFICIENT FUNDS]

Tenant agrees to pay a charge of ___ ___ ___ for each check given by Tenant to Landlord that is returned to landlord for lack of sufficient funds.

[SECURITY DEPOSIT]

Upon execution of this Lease, Tenant shall deposit the sum of ____________to be held by the Landlord as security deposit for reasonable repair of damages to, or cleaning of the Premises upon the expiration or termination of this Lease, or other notable damages.

[USE OF PREMISES]

1. Tenant agrees that the Premises shall be used and occupied for no other purpose than as dwelling and that the Premises shall be occupied only by Tenant and the following named adults _____________

____

_____________________________ and the following named children _______________

____

__________ and no other without first obtaining a written consent from the Landlord.

2. The tenant hereby agrees to be responsible for the following utilities and or services ___ ___ ___ _

__ ___ ___ ___ ___ ___ ___ ___ ___ ___ ___ ___ ___ ___________________

3. The Tenant is responsible for the following maintenance and or repairs ___ ___ ___ ___ ___ __

_ ___ ___ ___ ___ ___ ___ ___ ___ ___ ___ ___ ___ _____ ___ ___ ___

4. The tenant agrees not to keep any pets on the premises without priorly obtaining a written consent from the Landlord.

[ABANDONMENT AND RIGHT TO ENTER]

In any case that the Tenant abandons the Premises during the term of this Agreement, the Landlord has the right to enter the Premises by any means necessary without facing any liability and the Landlord may terminate this Agreement.

[AMENDMENTS]

The Landlord and Tenant agree that any amendments made to this Agreement must be in writing where they must be signed by both the Landlord and the Tenant. As such any amendment made by the parties will be applied to this Agreement.

[GOVERNING LAW]

This Agreement shall be governed by and construed in accordance with the laws of ___ ___ ___ ___

___ ___ ___ ___ ___ ___ ___ ___ ___ ___ ___ ___ ___ ___________________

TENANT

Name ___________________________

Signature _________________________

Date ____________________________

Witness __________________________

Phone ___________________________

Address __________________________

____

Signature ________________________

Date ____________________________

LANDLORD

Name _________________________

Signature _______________________

Date __________________________

Address ________________________

____

Witness ________________________

Phone __________________________

Address ________________________

Signature___________Date__________

MONTH-TO-MONTH RENTAL **AGREEMENT**

This lease agreement is made this ___________ by and (between/among) _______ ___ ___ ___ ___ ___ ___ [Landlord] and ___ ___ ___ ___ ___ ___, [and other Tenants,] collectively [Tenant]. Each Tenant is jointly and severally liable for the payment of rent to the landlord and performance of all other terms in this Agreement.

[PREMISES]

Landlord hereby leases the premises located at ___ ___ ___ ___ ___ ___ ___ ___ ___ ___ City of ___ ___ ___ ___ ___, State of ___ ___ ___ ___ ___ ___ ___ ___ [Premises] to Tenant.

[LEASE TERM]

The Lease will start on ___ of ___ ___ ___, 20 ___ and will continue as a month-to-month tenancy. To terminate tenancy, the Landlord or Tenant must give the other party a ___ ___ day written notice of lease non-renewal.

[LEASE PAYMENTS]

The Tenant agrees to pay Landlord for the use of the Premises in the amount of $ ___ __, payable in advance on the first day of each month, except when day falls on a legal holiday or weekend, in which case rent is due on the next business day. Rent will be paid to Landlord at Landlord's address provided herein (or to other places as directed by Landlord) by mail to ___ ___ ___ ___ ___ ___ ___ ___ ___ ___ _ __ ___ or in person, at ___ ___ ___ ___ ___ ___ ___ ___ ___ ___ ___ ___ ___ ___ ___ __.

Landlord will accept check made payable to ______________________________ _or cashier's check made payable to ______________________________________ __or payment by ___________________________ to___________________________

[LATE FEE]

Rent paid after the ___ ___ day of each month will be considered as late; and if rent is not paid within ___ ___ days of such due date, Tenant agrees to pay a late fee of ___ ___ ___ per day for every day that the rent is late.

[INSUFFICIENT FUNDS]

Tenant agrees to pay a charge of ___ ___ ___ for each check given by Tenant to Landlord that is returned to landlord for lack of sufficient funds.

[SECURITY DEPOSIT]

Upon execution of this Lease, Tenant shall deposit the sum of ____________to be held by the Landlord as security deposit for reasonable repair of damages to, or cleaning of the Premises upon the expiration or termination of this Lease, or other notable damages.

[USE OF PREMISES]

1. Tenant agrees that the Premises shall be used and occupied for no other purpose than as dwelling and that the Premises shall be occupied only by Tenant and the following named adults _____________

____

______________________________ and the following named children ______________

____

__________ and no other without first obtaining a written consent from the Landlord.

2. The tenant hereby agrees to be responsible for the following utilities and or services ___ ___ ___ _

__ ___ ___ ___ ___ ___ ___ ___ ___ ___ ___ ___ ___ ___ _________________

3. The Tenant is responsible for the following maintenance and or repairs ___ ___ ___ ___ ___ __

_ ___ ___ ___ ___ ___ ___ ___ ___ ___ ___ ___ ___ ______ ___ ___ ___

4. The tenant agrees not to keep any pets on the premises without priorly obtaining a written consent from the Landlord.

[ABANDONMENT AND RIGHT TO ENTER]

In any case that the Tenant abandons the Premises during the term of this Agreement, the Landlord has the right to enter the Premises by any means necessary without facing any liability and the Landlord may terminate this Agreement.

[AMENDMENTS]

The Landlord and Tenant agree that any amendments made to this Agreement must be in writing where they must be signed by both the Landlord and the Tenant. As such any amendment made by the parties will be applied to this Agreement.

[GOVERNING LAW]

This Agreement shall be governed by and construed in accordance with the laws of ___ ___ ___ ___

___ ___ ___ ___ ___ ___ ___ ___ ___ ___ ___ ____________________

TENANT

Name ____________________________

Signature ___________________________

Date ____________________________

Witness ___________________________

Phone ____________________________

Address ___________________________

____

Signature __________________________

Date ___________________________

LANDLORD

Name __________________________

Signature ________________________

Date _________________________

Address ________________________

____

Witness ________________________

Phone __________________________

Address ________________________

Signature____________Date__________

MONTH-TO-MONTH RENTAL AGREEMENT

This lease agreement is made this _ _ _ _ _ _ _ _ _ _ by and (between/among) _ [Landlord] and _ _ _ _ _ _ _ _ _ _ _ _ _ _ _ _ _ _ , [and other Tenants,] collectively [Tenant]. Each Tenant is jointly and severally liable for the payment of rent to the landlord and performance of all other terms in this Agreement.

[PREMISES]

Landlord hereby leases the premises located at _ City of _ _ _ _ _ _ _ _ _ _ _ _ _ _ _, State of _ [Premises] to Tenant.

[LEASE TERM]

The Lease will start on _ _ _ of _ _ _ _ _ _ _ _ _, 20 _ _ _ and will continue as a month-to-month tenancy. To terminate tenancy, the Landlord or Tenant must give the other party a _ _ _ _ _ _ day written notice of lease non-renewal.

[LEASE PAYMENTS]

The Tenant agrees to pay Landlord for the use of the Premises in the amount of $ _ _ _ _ _, payable in advance on the first day of each month, except when day falls on a legal holiday or weekend, in which case rent is due on the next business day. Rent will be paid to Landlord at Landlord's address provided herein (or to other places as directed by Landlord) by mail to _ or in person, at _ .

Landlord will accept check made payable to _ or cashier's check made payable to _ or payment by _ to _

[LATE FEE]

Rent paid after the _ _ _ _ _ _ day of each month will be considered as late; and if rent is not paid within _ _ _ _ _ _ days of such due date, Tenant agrees to pay a late fee of _ _ _ _ _ _ _ _ _ per day for every day that the rent is late.

[INSUFFICIENT FUNDS]

Tenant agrees to pay a charge of _ _ _ _ _ _ _ _ _ for each check given by Tenant to Landlord that is returned to landlord for lack of sufficient funds.

[SECURITY DEPOSIT]

Upon execution of this Lease, Tenant shall deposit the sum of _ _ _ _ _ _ _ _ _ _ _ _ _to be held by the Landlord as security deposit for reasonable repair of damages to, or cleaning of the Premises upon the expiration or termination of this Lease, or other notable damages.

[USE OF PREMISES]

1. Tenant agrees that the Premises shall be used and occupied for no other purpose than as dwelling and that the Premises shall be occupied only by Tenant and the following named adults _____________

____

______________________________ and the following named children ______________

____

__________ and no other without first obtaining a written consent from the Landlord.

2. The tenant hereby agrees to be responsible for the following utilities and or services ___ ___ ___ _

__ ___ ___ ___ ___ ___ ___ ___ ___ ___ ___ ___ ___ ___ _________________

3. The Tenant is responsible for the following maintenance and or repairs ___ ___ ___ ___ ___ __

_ ___ ___ ___ ___ ___ ___ ___ ___ ___ ___ ___ ___ _____ ___ ___ ___ ___

4. The tenant agrees not to keep any pets on the premises without priorly obtaining a written consent from the Landlord.

[ABANDONMENT AND RIGHT TO ENTER]

In any case that the Tenant abandons the Premises during the term of this Agreement, the Landlord has the right to enter the Premises by any means necessary without facing any liability and the Landlord may terminate this Agreement.

[AMENDMENTS]

The Landlord and Tenant agree that any amendments made to this Agreement must be in writing where they must be signed by both the Landlord and the Tenant. As such any amendment made by the parties will be applied to this Agreement.

[GOVERNING LAW]

This Agreement shall be governed by and construed in accordance with the laws of ___ ___ ___ ___

___ ___ ___ ___ ___ ___ ___ ___ ___ ___ ___ ___ ___ _________________

TENANT

Name ___________________________

Signature _________________________

Date ____________________________

Witness __________________________

Phone ___________________________

Address __________________________

____

Signature _________________________

Date ___________________________

LANDLORD

Name ___________________________

Signature _________________________

Date ____________________________

Address __________________________

____

Witness __________________________

Phone ___________________________

Address __________________________

Signature____________Date__________

MONTH-TO-MONTH RENTAL AGREEMENT

This lease agreement is made this ___________ by and (between/among) _______ ___ ___ ___ ___ ___ ___ [Landlord] and ___ ___ ___ ___ ___ ___, [and other Tenants,] collectively [Tenant]. Each Tenant is jointly and severally liable for the payment of rent to the landlord and performance of all other terms in this Agreement.

[PREMISES]

Landlord hereby leases the premises located at ___ ___ ___ ___ ___ ___ ___ ___ ___ ___ City of ___ ___ ___ ___ ___, State of ___ ___ ___ ___ ___ ___ ___ [Premises] to Tenant.

[LEASE TERM]

The Lease will start on ___ of ___ ___ ___, 20 ___ and will continue as a month-to-month tenancy. To terminate tenancy, the Landlord or Tenant must give the other party a ___ ___ day written notice of lease non-renewal.

[LEASE PAYMENTS]

The Tenant agrees to pay Landlord for the use of the Premises in the amount of $ ___ __, payable in advance on the first day of each month, except when day falls on a legal holiday or weekend, in which case rent is due on the next business day. Rent will be paid to Landlord at Landlord's address provided herein (or to other places as directed by Landlord) by mail to ___ ___ ___ ___ ___ ___ ___ ___ ___ ___ _ __ ___or in person, at ___ ___ ___ ___ ___ ___ ___ ___ ___ ___ ___ ___ ___ ___ __.
Landlord will accept check made payable to _______________________________________
_or cashier's check made payable to ____
__or payment by ___________________________ to___________________________

[LATE FEE]

Rent paid after the ___ ___ day of each month will be considered as late; and if rent is not paid within ___ ___ days of such due date, Tenant agrees to pay a late fee of ___ ___ ___ per day for every day that the rent is late.

[INSUFFICIENT FUNDS]

Tenant agrees to pay a charge of ___ ___ ___ for each check given by Tenant to Landlord that is returned to landlord for lack of sufficient funds.

[SECURITY DEPOSIT]

Upon execution of this Lease, Tenant shall deposit the sum of _____________to be held by the Landlord as security deposit for reasonable repair of damages to, or cleaning of the Premises upon the expiration or termination of this Lease, or other notable damages.

[USE OF PREMISES]

1. Tenant agrees that the Premises shall be used and occupied for no other purpose than as dwelling and that the Premises shall be occupied only by Tenant and the following named adults _____________

____

_____________________________ and the following named children ______________

____

__________ and no other without first obtaining a written consent from the Landlord.

2. The tenant hereby agrees to be responsible for the following utilities and or services ___ ___ ____ _

__ ___ ___ ___ ___ ___ ___ ___ ___ ___ ___ ___ ___ ________________

3. The Tenant is responsible for the following maintenance and or repairs ___ ___ ___ ___ ___ __

_ ___ ___ ___ ___ ___ ___ ___ ___ ___ ___ ___ ___ _____ ___ ___ ___ ___

4. The tenant agrees not to keep any pets on the premises without priorly obtaining a written consent from the Landlord.

[ABANDONMENT AND RIGHT TO ENTER]

In any case that the Tenant abandons the Premises during the term of this Agreement, the Landlord has the right to enter the Premises by any means necessary without facing any liability and the Landlord may terminate this Agreement.

[AMENDMENTS]

The Landlord and Tenant agree that any amendments made to this Agreement must be in writing where they must be signed by both the Landlord and the Tenant. As such any amendment made by the parties will be applied to this Agreement.

[GOVERNING LAW]

This Agreement shall be governed by and construed in accordance with the laws of ___ ___ ___ ___

___ ___ ___ ___ ___ ___ ___ ___ ___ ___ ___ ___ ___ ___ ___________________

TENANT

Name ____________________________

Signature __________________________

Date _____________________________

Witness ___________________________

Phone ____________________________

Address ___________________________

____

Signature _________________________

Date ____________________________

LANDLORD

Name ___________________________

Signature ________________________

Date ___________________________ _

Address _________________________

____

Witness _________________________

Phone ___________________________

Address _________________________

Signature___________Date__________

MONTH-TO-MONTH RENTAL AGREEMENT

This lease agreement is made this __________ by and (between/among) _______ ___ ___ ___
___ ___ ___ [Landlord] and ___ ___ ___ ___ ___ ___, [and other Tenants,] collectively [Tenant]. Each Tenant is jointly and severally liable for the payment of rent to the landlord and performance of all other terms in this Agreement.

[PREMISES]

Landlord hereby leases the premises located at ___ ___ ___ ___ ___ ___ ___ ___ ___ ___
City of ___ ___ ___ ___ ___, State of ___ ___ ___ ___ ___ ___ ___ ___ [Premises] to Tenant.

[LEASE TERM]

The Lease will start on ___ of ___ ___ ___, 20 ___ and will continue as a month-to-month tenancy. To terminate tenancy, the Landlord or Tenant must give the other party a ___ ___ day written notice of lease non-renewal.

[LEASE PAYMENTS]

The Tenant agrees to pay Landlord for the use of the Premises in the amount of $ ___ __, payable in advance on the first day of each month, except when day falls on a legal holiday or weekend, in which case rent is due on the next business day. Rent will be paid to Landlord at Landlord's address provided herein (or to other places as directed by Landlord) by mail to ___ ___ ___ ___ ___ ___ ___ ___ ___ ___ _
__ ___ or in person, at ___ ___ ___ ___ ___ ___ ___ ___ ___ ___ ___ ___ ___ __.
Landlord will accept check made payable to ______________________________
_or cashier's check made payable to _________________________________
__or payment by __________________________ to_________________________

[LATE FEE]

Rent paid after the ___ ___ day of each month will be considered as late; and if rent is not paid within ___ ___ days of such due date, Tenant agrees to pay a late fee of ___ ___ ___ per day for every day that the rent is late.

[INSUFFICIENT FUNDS]

Tenant agrees to pay a charge of ___ ___ ___ for each check given by Tenant to Landlord that is returned to landlord for lack of sufficient funds.

[SECURITY DEPOSIT]

Upon execution of this Lease, Tenant shall deposit the sum of _____________to be held by the Landlord as security deposit for reasonable repair of damages to, or cleaning of the Premises upon the expiration or termination of this Lease, or other notable damages.

[USE OF PREMISES]

1. Tenant agrees that the Premises shall be used and occupied for no other purpose than as dwelling and that the Premises shall be occupied only by Tenant and the following named adults _____________

____

______________________________ and the following named children _______________

____

__________ and no other without first obtaining a written consent from the Landlord.

2. The tenant hereby agrees to be responsible for the following utilities and or services ___ ___ ___ _

__ ___ ___ ___ ___ ___ ___ ___ ___ ___ ___ ___ ___ ___ ________________

3. The Tenant is responsible for the following maintenance and or repairs ___ ___ ___ ___ ___ __

_ ___ ___ ___ ___ ___ ___ ___ ___ ___ ___ ___ ___ _____ ___ ___ ___ ___

4. The tenant agrees not to keep any pets on the premises without priorly obtaining a written consent from the Landlord.

[ABANDONMENT AND RIGHT TO ENTER]

In any case that the Tenant abandons the Premises during the term of this Agreement, the Landlord has the right to enter the Premises by any means necessary without facing any liability and the Landlord may terminate this Agreement.

[AMENDMENTS]

The Landlord and Tenant agree that any amendments made to this Agreement must be in writing where they must be signed by both the Landlord and the Tenant. As such any amendment made by the parties will be applied to this Agreement.

[GOVERNING LAW]

This Agreement shall be governed by and construed in accordance with the laws of ___ ___ ___ ___

___ ___ ___ ___ ___ ___ ___ ___ ___ ___ ___ ___ ___ ___________________

TENANT

Name ___________________________

Signature _________________________

Date ____________________________

Witness __________________________

Phone ___________________________

Address __________________________

____

Signature ________________________

Date ___________________________

LANDLORD

Name _________________________

Signature _______________________

Date ________________________ _

Address ________________________

____

Witness ________________________

Phone __________________________

Address ________________________

Signature___________Date__________

MONTH-TO-MONTH RENTAL AGREEMENT

This lease agreement is made this __________ by and (between/among) _______ ___ ___ ___ ___ ___ ___ [Landlord] and ___ ___ ___ ___ ___ ___, [and other Tenants,] collectively [Tenant]. Each Tenant is jointly and severally liable for the payment of rent to the landlord and performance of all other terms in this Agreement.

[PREMISES]

Landlord hereby leases the premises located at ___ ___ ___ ___ ___ ___ ___ ___ ___ ___ City of ___ ___ ___ ___ ___, State of ___ ___ ___ ___ ___ ___ ___ ___ [Premises] to Tenant.

[LEASE TERM]

The Lease will start on ___ of ___ ___ ___, 20 ___ and will continue as a month-to-month tenancy. To terminate tenancy, the Landlord or Tenant must give the other party a ___ ___ day written notice of lease non-renewal.

[LEASE PAYMENTS]

The Tenant agrees to pay Landlord for the use of the Premises in the amount of $ ___ __, payable in advance on the first day of each month, except when day falls on a legal holiday or weekend, in which case rent is due on the next business day. Rent will be paid to Landlord at Landlord's address provided herein (or to other places as directed by Landlord) by mail to ___ ___ ___ ___ ___ ___ ___ ___ ___ ___ _ __ ___ or in person, at ___ ___ ___ ___ ___ ___ ___ ___ ___ ___ ___ ___ ___ ___ __. Landlord will accept check made payable to ______________________________________ _or cashier's check made payable to ____ __or payment by __________________________ to__________________________

[LATE FEE]

Rent paid after the ___ ___ day of each month will be considered as late; and if rent is not paid within ___ ___ days of such due date, Tenant agrees to pay a late fee of ___ ___ ___ per day for every day that the rent is late.

[INSUFFICIENT FUNDS]

Tenant agrees to pay a charge of ___ ___ ___ for each check given by Tenant to Landlord that is returned to landlord for lack of sufficient funds.

[SECURITY DEPOSIT]

Upon execution of this Lease, Tenant shall deposit the sum of _____________to be held by the Landlord as security deposit for reasonable repair of damages to, or cleaning of the Premises upon the expiration or termination of this Lease, or other notable damages.

[USE OF PREMISES]

1. Tenant agrees that the Premises shall be used and occupied for no other purpose than as dwelling and that the Premises shall be occupied only by Tenant and the following named adults _____________

____

_____________________________ and the following named children _______________

____

__________ and no other without first obtaining a written consent from the Landlord.

2. The tenant hereby agrees to be responsible for the following utilities and or services ___ ___ ___ _

__ ___ ___ ___ ___ ___ ___ ___ ___ ___ ___ ___ ___ ___ _________________

3. The Tenant is responsible for the following maintenance and or repairs ___ ___ ___ ___ ___ __

_ ___ ___ ___ ___ ___ ___ ___ ___ ___ ___ ___ ___ _____ ___ ___ ___ ___

4. The tenant agrees not to keep any pets on the premises without priorly obtaining a written consent from the Landlord.

[ABANDONMENT AND RIGHT TO ENTER]

In any case that the Tenant abandons the Premises during the term of this Agreement, the Landlord has the right to enter the Premises by any means necessary without facing any liability and the Landlord may terminate this Agreement.

[AMENDMENTS]

The Landlord and Tenant agree that any amendments made to this Agreement must be in writing where they must be signed by both the Landlord and the Tenant. As such any amendment made by the parties will be applied to this Agreement.

[GOVERNING LAW]

This Agreement shall be governed by and construed in accordance with the laws of ___ ___ ___ ___

___ ___ ___ ___ ___ ___ ___ ___ ___ ___ ___ ___ ___ ___ ___ __________________

TENANT

Name ___________________________

Signature _________________________

Date ____________________________

Witness __________________________

Phone ___________________________

Address __________________________

____

Signature ________________________

Date ____________________________

LANDLORD

Name ___________________________

Signature _________________________

Date __________________________ _

Address __________________________

____

Witness __________________________

Phone ___________________________

Address __________________________

Signature___________Date__________

MONTH-TO-MONTH RENTAL AGREEMENT

This lease agreement is made this __________ by and (between/among) _______ ___ ___ ___ ___ ___ ___ [Landlord] and ___ ___ ___ ___ ___ ___, [and other Tenants,] collectively [Tenant]. Each Tenant is jointly and severally liable for the payment of rent to the landlord and performance of all other terms in this Agreement.

[PREMISES]

Landlord hereby leases the premises located at ___ ___ ___ ___ ___ ___ ___ ___ ___ ___ City of ___ ___ ___ ___ ___, State of ___ ___ ___ ___ ___ ___ ___ [Premises] to Tenant.

[LEASE TERM]

The Lease will start on ___ of ___ ___ ___, 20 ___ and will continue as a month-to-month tenancy. To terminate tenancy, the Landlord or Tenant must give the other party a ___ ___ day written notice of lease non-renewal.

[LEASE PAYMENTS]

The Tenant agrees to pay Landlord for the use of the Premises in the amount of $ ___ __, payable in advance on the first day of each month, except when day falls on a legal holiday or weekend, in which case rent is due on the next business day. Rent will be paid to Landlord at Landlord's address provided herein (or to other places as directed by Landlord) by mail to ___ ___ ___ ___ ___ ___ ___ ___ ___ ____ _ __ ___ or in person, at ___ ___ ___ ___ ___ ___ ___ ___ ___ ___ ___ ___ __.

Landlord will accept check made payable to ____

_or cashier's check made payable to ____

__or payment by __________________________ to________________________

[LATE FEE]

Rent paid after the ___ ___ day of each month will be considered as late; and if rent is not paid within ___ ___ days of such due date, Tenant agrees to pay a late fee of ___ ___ ___ per day for every day that the rent is late.

[INSUFFICIENT FUNDS]

Tenant agrees to pay a charge of ___ ___ ___ for each check given by Tenant to Landlord that is returned to landlord for lack of sufficient funds.

[SECURITY DEPOSIT]

Upon execution of this Lease, Tenant shall deposit the sum of _____________to be held by the Landlord as security deposit for reasonable repair of damages to, or cleaning of the Premises upon the expiration or termination of this Lease, or other notable damages.

[USE OF PREMISES]

1. Tenant agrees that the Premises shall be used and occupied for no other purpose than as dwelling and that the Premises shall be occupied only by Tenant and the following named adults _____________

____

_____________________________ and the following named children _______________

____

__________ and no other without first obtaining a written consent from the Landlord.

2. The tenant hereby agrees to be responsible for the following utilities and or services ___ ___ ____ _

____

3. The Tenant is responsible for the following maintenance and or repairs ___ ___ ___ ___ ___ __

____

4. The tenant agrees not to keep any pets on the premises without priorly obtaining a written consent from the Landlord.

[ABANDONMENT AND RIGHT TO ENTER]

In any case that the Tenant abandons the Premises during the term of this Agreement, the Landlord has the right to enter the Premises by any means necessary without facing any liability and the Landlord may terminate this Agreement.

[AMENDMENTS]

The Landlord and Tenant agree that any amendments made to this Agreement must be in writing where they must be signed by both the Landlord and the Tenant. As such any amendment made by the parties will be applied to this Agreement.

[GOVERNING LAW]

This Agreement shall be governed by and construed in accordance with the laws of ___ ___ ___ ___

____

TENANT

Name ____________________________

Signature __________________________

Date ______________________________

Witness ____________________________

Phone _____________________________

Address ____________________________

____

Signature __________________________

Date ______________________________

LANDLORD

Name ____________________________

Signature __________________________

Date ______________________________

Address ____________________________

____

Witness ____________________________

Phone _____________________________

Address ____________________________

Signature____________Date__________

MONTH-TO-MONTH RENTAL AGREEMENT

This lease agreement is made this __________ by and (between/among) _______ ___ ___ ___ ___ ___ ___ [Landlord] and ___ ___ ___ ___ ___ ___ , [and other Tenants,] collectively [Tenant]. Each Tenant is jointly and severally liable for the payment of rent to the landlord and performance of all other terms in this Agreement.

[PREMISES]

Landlord hereby leases the premises located at ___ ___ ___ ___ ___ ___ ___ ___ ___ ___ City of ___ ___ ___ ___ ___, State of ___ ___ ___ ___ ___ ___ ___ [Premises] to Tenant.

[LEASE TERM]

The Lease will start on ___ of ___ ___ ___, 20 ___ and will continue as a month-to-month tenancy. To terminate tenancy, the Landlord or Tenant must give the other party a ___ ___ day written notice of lease non-renewal.

[LEASE PAYMENTS]

The Tenant agrees to pay Landlord for the use of the Premises in the amount of $ ___ __, payable in advance on the first day of each month, except when day falls on a legal holiday or weekend, in which case rent is due on the next business day. Rent will be paid to Landlord at Landlord's address provided herein (or to other places as directed by Landlord) by mail to ___ ___ ___ ___ ___ ___ ___ ___ ___ ___ __ ___or in person, at ___ ___ ___ ___ ___ ___ ___ ___ ___ ___ ___ ___ __.

Landlord will accept check made payable to ______________________________ _or cashier's check made payable to ______________________________ __or payment by ___________________________ to_________________________

[LATE FEE]

Rent paid after the ___ ___ day of each month will be considered as late; and if rent is not paid within ___ ___ days of such due date, Tenant agrees to pay a late fee of ___ ___ ___ per day for every day that the rent is late.

[INSUFFICIENT FUNDS]

Tenant agrees to pay a charge of ___ ___ ___ for each check given by Tenant to Landlord that is returned to landlord for lack of sufficient funds.

[SECURITY DEPOSIT]

Upon execution of this Lease, Tenant shall deposit the sum of _____________to be held by the Landlord as security deposit for reasonable repair of damages to, or cleaning of the Premises upon the expiration or termination of this Lease, or other notable damages.

[USE OF PREMISES]

1. Tenant agrees that the Premises shall be used and occupied for no other purpose than as dwelling and that the Premises shall be occupied only by Tenant and the following named adults _____________

____

______________________________ and the following named children _______________

____

__________ and no other without first obtaining a written consent from the Landlord.

2. The tenant hereby agrees to be responsible for the following utilities and or services ___ ___ ___ _

__ ___ ___ ___ ___ ___ ___ ___ ___ ___ ___ ___ ___ ___ ___ _______________

3. The Tenant is responsible for the following maintenance and or repairs ___ ___ ___ ___ ___ __

_ ___ ___ ___ ___ ___ ___ ___ ___ ___ ___ ___ ___ ___ ___ _____ ___ ___ ___

4. The tenant agrees not to keep any pets on the premises without priorly obtaining a written consent from the Landlord.

[ABANDONMENT AND RIGHT TO ENTER]

In any case that the Tenant abandons the Premises during the term of this Agreement, the Landlord has the right to enter the Premises by any means necessary without facing any liability and the Landlord may terminate this Agreement.

[AMENDMENTS]

The Landlord and Tenant agree that any amendments made to this Agreement must be in writing where they must be signed by both the Landlord and the Tenant. As such any amendment made by the parties will be applied to this Agreement.

[GOVERNING LAW]

This Agreement shall be governed by and construed in accordance with the laws of ___ ___ ___ ___

___ ___ ___ ___ ___ ___ ___ ___ ___ ___ ___ ___ ___ ___ ____________________

TENANT

Name ____________________________

Signature __________________________

Date ______________________________

Witness ____________________________

Phone _____________________________

Address ____________________________

____

Signature _________________________

Date ____________________________

LANDLORD

Name ____________________________

Signature __________________________

Date ___________________________ _

Address ___________________________

____

Witness ___________________________

Phone _____________________________

Address ___________________________

Signature____________Date___________

MONTH-TO-MONTH RENTAL AGREEMENT

This lease agreement is made this _ _ _ _ _ _ _ _ _ _ by and (between/among) _ [Landlord] and _ , [and other Tenants,] collectively [Tenant]. Each Tenant is jointly and severally liable for the payment of rent to the landlord and performance of all other terms in this Agreement.

[PREMISES]

Landlord hereby leases the premises located at _ City of _ _ _ _ _ _ _ _ _ _ _ _ _ _ _ , State of _ [Premises] to Tenant.

[LEASE TERM]

The Lease will start on _ _ _ of _ _ _ _ _ _ _ _ _ , 20 _ _ _ and will continue as a month-to-month tenancy. To terminate tenancy, the Landlord or Tenant must give the other party a _ _ _ _ _ _ day written notice of lease non-renewal.

[LEASE PAYMENTS]

The Tenant agrees to pay Landlord for the use of the Premises in the amount of $ _ _ _ _ _, payable in advance on the first day of each month, except when day falls on a legal holiday or weekend, in which case rent is due on the next business day. Rent will be paid to Landlord at Landlord's address provided herein (or to other places as directed by Landlord) by mail to _ or in person, at _.

Landlord will accept check made payable to _

_or cashier's check made payable to _

_ _or payment by _ to_ _

[LATE FEE]

Rent paid after the _ _ _ _ _ _ day of each month will be considered as late; and if rent is not paid within _ _ _ _ _ _ days of such due date, Tenant agrees to pay a late fee of _ _ _ _ _ _ _ _ _ per day for every day that the rent is late.

[INSUFFICIENT FUNDS]

Tenant agrees to pay a charge of _ _ _ _ _ _ _ _ _ for each check given by Tenant to Landlord that is returned to landlord for lack of sufficient funds.

[SECURITY DEPOSIT]

Upon execution of this Lease, Tenant shall deposit the sum of _ _ _ _ _ _ _ _ _ _ _ _ _to be held by the Landlord as security deposit for reasonable repair of damages to, or cleaning of the Premises upon the expiration or termination of this Lease, or other notable damages.

[USE OF PREMISES]

1. Tenant agrees that the Premises shall be used and occupied for no other purpose than as dwelling and that the Premises shall be occupied only by Tenant and the following named adults ______________

____

______________________________ and the following named children ______________

____

__________ and no other without first obtaining a written consent from the Landlord.

2. The tenant hereby agrees to be responsible for the following utilities and or services ___ ___ ___ _

____

3. The Tenant is responsible for the following maintenance and or repairs ___ ___ ___ ___ ___ __

____

4. The tenant agrees not to keep any pets on the premises without priorly obtaining a written consent from the Landlord.

[ABANDONMENT AND RIGHT TO ENTER]

In any case that the Tenant abandons the Premises during the term of this Agreement, the Landlord has the right to enter the Premises by any means necessary without facing any liability and the Landlord may terminate this Agreement.

[AMENDMENTS]

The Landlord and Tenant agree that any amendments made to this Agreement must be in writing where they must be signed by both the Landlord and the Tenant. As such any amendment made by the parties will be applied to this Agreement.

[GOVERNING LAW]

This Agreement shall be governed by and construed in accordance with the laws of ___ ___ ___ ___

____

TENANT

Name ____________________________

Signature __________________________

Date _____________________________

Witness ___________________________

Phone ____________________________

Address ___________________________

____

Signature __________________________

Date _____________________________

LANDLORD

Name ____________________________

Signature __________________________

Date _____________________________

Address ___________________________

____

Witness ___________________________

Phone ____________________________

Address ___________________________

Signature____________Date__________

MONTH-TO-MONTH RENTAL AGREEMENT

This lease agreement is made this __________ by and (between/among) _______ ___ ___ ___ ___ ___ ___ [Landlord] and ___ ___ ___ ___ ___ ___, [and other Tenants,] collectively [Tenant]. Each Tenant is jointly and severally liable for the payment of rent to the landlord and performance of all other terms in this Agreement.

[PREMISES]

Landlord hereby leases the premises located at ___ ___ ___ ___ ___ ___ ___ ___ ___ ___ ___ City of ___ ___ ___ ___ ___, State of ___ ___ ___ ___ ___ ___ ___ [Premises] to Tenant.

[LEASE TERM]

The Lease will start on ___ of ___ ___ ___, 20 ___ and will continue as a month-to-month tenancy. To terminate tenancy, the Landlord or Tenant must give the other party a ___ ___ day written notice of lease non-renewal.

[LEASE PAYMENTS]

The Tenant agrees to pay Landlord for the use of the Premises in the amount of $ ___ __, payable in advance on the first day of each month, except when day falls on a legal holiday or weekend, in which case rent is due on the next business day. Rent will be paid to Landlord at Landlord's address provided herein (or to other places as directed by Landlord) by mail to ___ ___ ___ ___ ___ ___ ___ ___ ___ ___ _ __ ___ or in person, at ___ ___ ___ ___ ___ ___ ___ ___ ___ ___ ___ ___ ___ ___ __.
Landlord will accept check made payable to ______________________________
_or cashier's check made payable to ______________________________
__or payment by ___________________________ to_________________________

[LATE FEE]

Rent paid after the ___ ___ day of each month will be considered as late; and if rent is not paid within ___ ___ days of such due date, Tenant agrees to pay a late fee of ___ ___ ___ per day for every day that the rent is late.

[INSUFFICIENT FUNDS]

Tenant agrees to pay a charge of ___ ___ ___ for each check given by Tenant to Landlord that is returned to landlord for lack of sufficient funds.

[SECURITY DEPOSIT]

Upon execution of this Lease, Tenant shall deposit the sum of _____________to be held by the Landlord as security deposit for reasonable repair of damages to, or cleaning of the Premises upon the expiration or termination of this Lease, or other notable damages.

[USE OF PREMISES]

1. Tenant agrees that the Premises shall be used and occupied for no other purpose than as dwelling and that the Premises shall be occupied only by Tenant and the following named adults _____________

____

______________________________ and the following named children _______________

____

__________ and no other without first obtaining a written consent from the Landlord.

2. The tenant hereby agrees to be responsible for the following utilities and or services ___ ___ ___ _

__ ___ ___ ___ ___ ___ ___ ___ ___ ___ ___ ___ ___ ___ _________________

3. The Tenant is responsible for the following maintenance and or repairs ___ ___ ___ ___ ___ __

_ ___ ___ ___ ___ ___ ___ ___ ___ ___ ___ ___ ___ ____ ____ ___ ___ ___

4. The tenant agrees not to keep any pets on the premises without priorly obtaining a written consent from the Landlord.

[ABANDONMENT AND RIGHT TO ENTER]

In any case that the Tenant abandons the Premises during the term of this Agreement, the Landlord has the right to enter the Premises by any means necessary without facing any liability and the Landlord may terminate this Agreement.

[AMENDMENTS]

The Landlord and Tenant agree that any amendments made to this Agreement must be in writing where they must be signed by both the Landlord and the Tenant. As such any amendment made by the parties will be applied to this Agreement.

[GOVERNING LAW]

This Agreement shall be governed by and construed in accordance with the laws of ___ ___ ___ ___

___ ___ ___ ___ ___ ___ ___ ___ ___ ___ ___ ___ ___ ______________________

TENANT

Name ____________________________

Signature __________________________

Date ______________________________

Witness ____________________________

Phone _____________________________

Address ____________________________

____

Signature __________________________

Date ______________________________

LANDLORD

Name ____________________________

Signature __________________________

Date ___________________________

Address ___________________________

____

Witness ___________________________

Phone ____________________________

Address ___________________________

Signature____________Date___________

MONTH-TO-MONTH RENTAL **AGREEMENT**

This lease agreement is made this __________ by and (between/among) _______ ___ ___ ___ ___ ___ ___ [Landlord] and ___ ___ ___ ___ ___ ___, [and other Tenants,] collectively [Tenant]. Each Tenant is jointly and severally liable for the payment of rent to the landlord and performance of all other terms in this Agreement.

[PREMISES]

Landlord hereby leases the premises located at ___ ___ ___ ___ ___ ___ ___ ___ ___ ___

City of ___ ___ ___ ___ ___, State of ___ ___ ___ ___ ___ ___ ___ [Premises] to Tenant.

[LEASE TERM]

The Lease will start on ___ of ___ ___ ___, 20 ___ and will continue as a month-to-month tenancy. To terminate tenancy, the Landlord or Tenant must give the other party a ___ ___ day written notice of lease non-renewal.

[LEASE PAYMENTS]

The Tenant agrees to pay Landlord for the use of the Premises in the amount of $ ___ __, payable in advance on the first day of each month, except when day falls on a legal holiday or weekend, in which case rent is due on the next business day. Rent will be paid to Landlord at Landlord's address provided herein (or to other places as directed by Landlord) by mail to ___ ___ ___ ___ ___ ___ ___ ___ ___ ___ _ __ ___ or in person, at ___ ___ ___ ___ ___ ___ ___ ___ ___ ___ ___ ___ ___ ___ ___.

Landlord will accept check made payable to ______________________________

_or cashier's check made payable to ______________________________

__or payment by ___________________________ to___________________________

[LATE FEE]

Rent paid after the ___ ___ day of each month will be considered as late; and if rent is not paid within ___ ___ days of such due date, Tenant agrees to pay a late fee of ___ ___ ___ per day for every day that the rent is late.

[INSUFFICIENT FUNDS]

Tenant agrees to pay a charge of ___ ___ ___ for each check given by Tenant to Landlord that is returned to landlord for lack of sufficient funds.

[SECURITY DEPOSIT]

Upon execution of this Lease, Tenant shall deposit the sum of _____________to be held by the Landlord as security deposit for reasonable repair of damages to, or cleaning of the Premises upon the expiration or termination of this Lease, or other notable damages.

[USE OF PREMISES]

1. Tenant agrees that the Premises shall be used and occupied for no other purpose than as dwelling and that the Premises shall be occupied only by Tenant and the following named adults _____________

____

_____________________________ and the following named children _______________

____

__________ and no other without first obtaining a written consent from the Landlord.

2. The tenant hereby agrees to be responsible for the following utilities and or services ___ ___ ___ _

__ ___ ___ ___ ___ ___ ___ ___ ___ ___ ___ ___ ___ ___ _________________

3. The Tenant is responsible for the following maintenance and or repairs ___ ___ ___ ___ ___ __

_ ___ ___ ___ ___ ___ ___ ___ ___ ___ ___ ___ ___ _____ ___ ___ ___ ___

4. The tenant agrees not to keep any pets on the premises without priorly obtaining a written consent from the Landlord.

[ABANDONMENT AND RIGHT TO ENTER]

In any case that the Tenant abandons the Premises during the term of this Agreement, the Landlord has the right to enter the Premises by any means necessary without facing any liability and the Landlord may terminate this Agreement.

[AMENDMENTS]

The Landlord and Tenant agree that any amendments made to this Agreement must be in writing where they must be signed by both the Landlord and the Tenant. As such any amendment made by the parties will be applied to this Agreement.

[GOVERNING LAW]

This Agreement shall be governed by and construed in accordance with the laws of ___ ___ ___ ___

___ ___ ___ ___ ___ ___ ___ ___ ___ ___ ___ ___ ___ ___ ___ ___________________

TENANT

Name ____________________________

Signature _________________________

Date _____________________________

Witness ___________________________

Phone ____________________________

Address ___________________________

____

Signature _________________________

Date _____________________________

LANDLORD

Name ____________________________

Signature _________________________

Date _____________________________

Address ___________________________

____

Witness ___________________________

Phone ____________________________

Address ___________________________

Signature___________Date__________

MONTH-TO-MONTH RENTAL **AGREEMENT**

This lease agreement is made this __________ by and (between/among) _______ ___ ___ ___ ___ ___ ___ [Landlord] and ___ ___ ___ ___ ___ ___, [and other Tenants,] collectively [Tenant]. Each Tenant is jointly and severally liable for the payment of rent to the landlord and performance of all other terms in this Agreement.

[PREMISES]

Landlord hereby leases the premises located at ___ ___ ___ ___ ___ ___ ___ ___ ___ ___ City of ___ ___ ___ ___ ___, State of ___ ___ ___ ___ ___ ___ ___ ___ [Premises] to Tenant.

[LEASE TERM]

The Lease will start on ___ of ___ ___ ___, 20 ___ and will continue as a month-to-month tenancy. To terminate tenancy, the Landlord or Tenant must give the other party a ___ ___ day written notice of lease non-renewal.

[LEASE PAYMENTS]

The Tenant agrees to pay Landlord for the use of the Premises in the amount of $ ___ __, payable in advance on the first day of each month, except when day falls on a legal holiday or weekend, in which case rent is due on the next business day. Rent will be paid to Landlord at Landlord's address provided herein (or to other places as directed by Landlord) by mail to ___ ___ ___ ___ ___ ___ ___ ___ ___ ___ _ __ ___ or in person, at ___ ___ ___ ___ ___ ___ ___ ___ ___ ___ ___ ___ ___ ___ __. Landlord will accept check made payable to ______________________________ _or cashier's check made payable to ______________________________ __or payment by ________________________ to__________________________

[LATE FEE]

Rent paid after the ___ ___ day of each month will be considered as late; and if rent is not paid within ___ ___ days of such due date, Tenant agrees to pay a late fee of ___ ___ ___ per day for every day that the rent is late.

[INSUFFICIENT FUNDS]

Tenant agrees to pay a charge of ___ ___ ___ for each check given by Tenant to Landlord that is returned to landlord for lack of sufficient funds.

[SECURITY DEPOSIT]

Upon execution of this Lease, Tenant shall deposit the sum of _____________to be held by the Landlord as security deposit for reasonable repair of damages to, or cleaning of the Premises upon the expiration or termination of this Lease, or other notable damages.

[USE OF PREMISES]

1. Tenant agrees that the Premises shall be used and occupied for no other purpose than as dwelling and that the Premises shall be occupied only by Tenant and the following named adults _____________

____

______________________________ and the following named children ________________

____

__________ and no other without first obtaining a written consent from the Landlord.

2. The tenant hereby agrees to be responsible for the following utilities and or services ___ ___ ___ _

__ ___ ___ ___ ___ ___ ___ ___ ___ ___ ___ ___ ___ _________________

3. The Tenant is responsible for the following maintenance and or repairs ___ ___ ___ ___ ___ __

_ ___ ___ ___ ___ ___ ___ ___ ___ ___ ___ ___ ___ _____ ___ ___ ___ ___

4. The tenant agrees not to keep any pets on the premises without priorly obtaining a written consent from the Landlord.

[ABANDONMENT AND RIGHT TO ENTER]

In any case that the Tenant abandons the Premises during the term of this Agreement, the Landlord has the right to enter the Premises by any means necessary without facing any liability and the Landlord may terminate this Agreement.

[AMENDMENTS]

The Landlord and Tenant agree that any amendments made to this Agreement must be in writing where they must be signed by both the Landlord and the Tenant. As such any amendment made by the parties will be applied to this Agreement.

[GOVERNING LAW]

This Agreement shall be governed by and construed in accordance with the laws of ___ ___ ___ ___

___ ___ ___ ___ ___ ___ ___ ___ ___ ___ ___ ___ ___ ____________________

TENANT

Name ____________________________

Signature _________________________

Date _____________________________

Witness ___________________________

Phone ____________________________

Address ___________________________

____

Signature _________________________

Date _____________________________

LANDLORD

Name ____________________________

Signature _________________________

Date ___________________________ _

Address ___________________________

____

Witness ___________________________

Phone ____________________________

Address ___________________________

Signature___________Date__________

MONTH-TO-MONTH RENTAL **AGREEMENT**

This lease agreement is made this __________ by and (between/among) _______ ___ ___ ___ ___ ___ ___ [Landlord] and ___ ___ ___ ___ ___ ___, [and other Tenants,] collectively [Tenant]. Each Tenant is jointly and severally liable for the payment of rent to the landlord and performance of all other terms in this Agreement.

[PREMISES]

Landlord hereby leases the premises located at ___ ___ ___ ___ ___ ___ ___ ___ ___ ___ City of ___ ___ ___ ___ ___, State of ___ ___ ___ ___ ___ ___ ___ ___ [Premises] to Tenant.

[LEASE TERM]

The Lease will start on ___ of ___ ___ ___, 20 ___ and will continue as a month-to-month tenancy. To terminate tenancy, the Landlord or Tenant must give the other party a ___ ___ day written notice of lease non-renewal.

[LEASE PAYMENTS]

The Tenant agrees to pay Landlord for the use of the Premises in the amount of $ ___ __, payable in advance on the first day of each month, except when day falls on a legal holiday or weekend, in which case rent is due on the next business day. Rent will be paid to Landlord at Landlord's address provided herein (or to other places as directed by Landlord) by mail to ___ ___ ___ ___ ___ ___ ___ ___ ___ ___ _ __ ___ or in person, at ___ ___ ___ ___ ___ ___ ___ ___ ___ ___ ___ ___ ___ __.

Landlord will accept check made payable to _______________________________________

_or cashier's check made payable to _______________________________________

__or payment by __________________________ to_________________________

[LATE FEE]

Rent paid after the ___ ___ day of each month will be considered as late; and if rent is not paid within ___ ___ days of such due date, Tenant agrees to pay a late fee of ___ ___ ___ per day for every day that the rent is late.

[INSUFFICIENT FUNDS]

Tenant agrees to pay a charge of ___ ___ ___ for each check given by Tenant to Landlord that is returned to landlord for lack of sufficient funds.

[SECURITY DEPOSIT]

Upon execution of this Lease, Tenant shall deposit the sum of ____________to be held by the Landlord as security deposit for reasonable repair of damages to, or cleaning of the Premises upon the expiration or termination of this Lease, or other notable damages.

[USE OF PREMISES]

1. Tenant agrees that the Premises shall be used and occupied for no other purpose than as dwelling and that the Premises shall be occupied only by Tenant and the following named adults _____________

____

______________________________ and the following named children ________________

____

__________ and no other without first obtaining a written consent from the Landlord.

2. The tenant hereby agrees to be responsible for the following utilities and or services ___ ___ ___ _

__ ___ ___ ___ ___ ___ ___ ___ ___ ___ ___ ___ ___ ___ ___________________

3. The Tenant is responsible for the following maintenance and or repairs ___ ___ ___ ___ ___ __

_ ___ ___ ___ ___ ___ ___ ___ ___ ___ ___ ___ ___ _____ ___ ___ ___ ___

4. The tenant agrees not to keep any pets on the premises without priorly obtaining a written consent from the Landlord.

[ABANDONMENT AND RIGHT TO ENTER]

In any case that the Tenant abandons the Premises during the term of this Agreement, the Landlord has the right to enter the Premises by any means necessary without facing any liability and the Landlord may terminate this Agreement.

[AMENDMENTS]

The Landlord and Tenant agree that any amendments made to this Agreement must be in writing where they must be signed by both the Landlord and the Tenant. As such any amendment made by the parties will be applied to this Agreement.

[GOVERNING LAW]

This Agreement shall be governed by and construed in accordance with the laws of ___ ___ ___ ___

___ ___ ___ ___ ___ ___ ___ ___ ___ ___ ___ ___ ___ ___ ___________________

TENANT

Name ___________________________

Signature _________________________

Date ____________________________

Witness __________________________

Phone ____________________________

Address __________________________

____

Signature ________________________

Date ___________________________

LANDLORD

Name ___________________________

Signature _________________________

Date ___________________________ _

Address ___________________________

____

Witness ___________________________

Phone _____________________________

Address ___________________________

Signature___________Date__________

MONTH-TO-MONTH RENTAL **AGREEMENT**

This lease agreement is made this __________ by and (between/among) _______ ___ ___ ___ ___ ___ ___ [Landlord] and ___ ___ ___ ___ ___ ___ , [and other Tenants,] collectively [Tenant]. Each Tenant is jointly and severally liable for the payment of rent to the landlord and performance of all other terms in this Agreement.

[PREMISES]

Landlord hereby leases the premises located at ___ ___ ___ ___ ___ ___ ___ ___ ___ ___ City of ___ ___ ___ ___ ___ , State of ___ ___ ___ ___ ___ ___ ___ [Premises] to Tenant.

[LEASE TERM]

The Lease will start on ___ of ___ ___ ___ , 20 ___ and will continue as a month-to-month tenancy. To terminate tenancy, the Landlord or Tenant must give the other party a ___ ___ day written notice of lease non-renewal.

[LEASE PAYMENTS]

The Tenant agrees to pay Landlord for the use of the Premises in the amount of $ ___ __, payable in advance on the first day of each month, except when day falls on a legal holiday or weekend, in which case rent is due on the next business day. Rent will be paid to Landlord at Landlord's address provided herein (or to other places as directed by Landlord) by mail to ___ ___ ___ ___ ___ ___ ___ ___ ___ ___ _ __ ___ or in person, at ___ ___ ___ ___ ___ ___ ___ ___ ___ ___ ___ ___ ___ ___ __.

Landlord will accept check made payable to ____

_or cashier's check made payable to ____

__or payment by ___________________________to__________________________

[LATE FEE]

Rent paid after the ___ ___ day of each month will be considered as late; and if rent is not paid within ___ ___ days of such due date, Tenant agrees to pay a late fee of ___ ___ ___ per day for every day that the rent is late.

[INSUFFICIENT FUNDS]

Tenant agrees to pay a charge of ___ ___ ___ for each check given by Tenant to Landlord that is returned to landlord for lack of sufficient funds.

[SECURITY DEPOSIT]

Upon execution of this Lease, Tenant shall deposit the sum of _____________to be held by the Landlord as security deposit for reasonable repair of damages to, or cleaning of the Premises upon the expiration or termination of this Lease, or other notable damages.

[USE OF PREMISES]

1. Tenant agrees that the Premises shall be used and occupied for no other purpose than as dwelling and that the Premises shall be occupied only by Tenant and the following named adults _____________

____

____________________________ and the following named children ______________

____

__________ and no other without first obtaining a written consent from the Landlord.

2. The tenant hereby agrees to be responsible for the following utilities and or services ___ ___ ___ _

__ ___ ___ ___ ___ ___ ___ ___ ___ ___ ___ ___ ___ ________________

3. The Tenant is responsible for the following maintenance and or repairs ___ ___ ___ ___ ___ __

_ ___ ___ ___ ___ ___ ___ ___ ___ ___ ___ ___ ___ _____ ___ ___ ___ ___

4. The tenant agrees not to keep any pets on the premises without priorly obtaining a written consent from the Landlord.

[ABANDONMENT AND RIGHT TO ENTER]

In any case that the Tenant abandons the Premises during the term of this Agreement, the Landlord has the right to enter the Premises by any means necessary without facing any liability and the Landlord may terminate this Agreement.

[AMENDMENTS]

The Landlord and Tenant agree that any amendments made to this Agreement must be in writing where they must be signed by both the Landlord and the Tenant. As such any amendment made by the parties will be applied to this Agreement.

[GOVERNING LAW]

This Agreement shall be governed by and construed in accordance with the laws of ___ ___ ___ ___

___ ___ ___ ___ ___ ___ ___ ___ ___ ___ ___ ___ ___ __________________

TENANT

Name ____________________________

Signature _________________________

Date _____________________________

Witness ___________________________

Phone ____________________________

Address ___________________________

____

Signature ________________________

Date ____________________________

LANDLORD

Name ___________________________

Signature ________________________

Date ___________________________

Address _________________________

____

Witness _________________________

Phone ___________________________

Address _________________________

Signature___________Date__________

MONTH-TO-MONTH RENTAL **AGREEMENT**

This lease agreement is made this __________ by and (between/among) _______ ___ ___ ___ ___ ___ ___ [Landlord] and ___ ___ ___ ___ ___ ___, [and other Tenants,] collectively [Tenant]. Each Tenant is jointly and severally liable for the payment of rent to the landlord and performance of all other terms in this Agreement.

[PREMISES]

Landlord hereby leases the premises located at ___ ___ ___ ___ ___ ___ ___ ___ ___ ___

City of ___ ___ ___ ___ ___, State of ___ ___ ___ ___ ___ ___ ___ ___ [Premises] to Tenant.

[LEASE TERM]

The Lease will start on ___ of ___ ___ ___, 20 ___ and will continue as a month-to-month tenancy. To terminate tenancy, the Landlord or Tenant must give the other party a ___ ___ day written notice of lease non-renewal.

[LEASE PAYMENTS]

The Tenant agrees to pay Landlord for the use of the Premises in the amount of $ ___ __, payable in advance on the first day of each month, except when day falls on a legal holiday or weekend, in which case rent is due on the next business day. Rent will be paid to Landlord at Landlord's address provided herein (or to other places as directed by Landlord) by mail to ___ ___ ___ ___ ___ ___ ___ ___ ___ ___ _
__ ___ or in person, at ___ ___ ___ ___ ___ ___ ___ ___ ___ ___ ___ ___ ___ ___ __.
Landlord will accept check made payable to ___________________________________
_or cashier's check made payable to ____
__or payment by ___________________________ to_________________________

[LATE FEE]

Rent paid after the ___ ___ day of each month will be considered as late; and if rent is not paid within ___ ___ days of such due date, Tenant agrees to pay a late fee of ___ ___ ___ per day for every day that the rent is late.

[INSUFFICIENT FUNDS]

Tenant agrees to pay a charge of ___ ___ ___ for each check given by Tenant to Landlord that is returned to landlord for lack of sufficient funds.

[SECURITY DEPOSIT]

Upon execution of this Lease, Tenant shall deposit the sum of _____________to be held by the Landlord as security deposit for reasonable repair of damages to, or cleaning of the Premises upon the expiration or termination of this Lease, or other notable damages.

[USE OF PREMISES]

1. Tenant agrees that the Premises shall be used and occupied for no other purpose than as dwelling and that the Premises shall be occupied only by Tenant and the following named adults _____________

____

_____________________________ and the following named children ______________

____

__________ and no other without first obtaining a written consent from the Landlord.

2. The tenant hereby agrees to be responsible for the following utilities and or services ___ ___ ___ _

__ ___ ___ ___ ___ ___ ___ ___ ___ ___ ___ ___ ___ ___ ________________

3. The Tenant is responsible for the following maintenance and or repairs ___ ___ ___ ___ ___ __

_ ___ ___ ___ ___ ___ ___ ___ ___ ___ ___ ___ ___ _____ ___ ___ ___ ___

4. The tenant agrees not to keep any pets on the premises without priorly obtaining a written consent from the Landlord.

[ABANDONMENT AND RIGHT TO ENTER]

In any case that the Tenant abandons the Premises during the term of this Agreement, the Landlord has the right to enter the Premises by any means necessary without facing any liability and the Landlord may terminate this Agreement.

[AMENDMENTS]

The Landlord and Tenant agree that any amendments made to this Agreement must be in writing where they must be signed by both the Landlord and the Tenant. As such any amendment made by the parties will be applied to this Agreement.

[GOVERNING LAW]

This Agreement shall be governed by and construed in accordance with the laws of ___ ___ ___ ___

___ ___ ___ ___ ___ ___ ___ ___ ___ ___ ___ ___ ___ ___ ________________

TENANT

Name ___________________________

Signature ________________________

Date ____________________________

Witness __________________________

Phone ___________________________

Address __________________________

____

Signature ________________________

Date ___________________________

LANDLORD

Name ___________________________

Signature ________________________

Date _________________________ _

Address __________________________

____

Witness __________________________

Phone ___________________________

Address __________________________

Signature___________Date__________

MONTH-TO-MONTH RENTAL AGREEMENT

This lease agreement is made this __________ by and (between/among) _______ ___ ___ ___ ___ ___ ___ [Landlord] and ___ ___ ___ ___ ___ ___, [and other Tenants,] collectively [Tenant]. Each Tenant is jointly and severally liable for the payment of rent to the landlord and performance of all other terms in this Agreement.

[PREMISES]

Landlord hereby leases the premises located at ___ ___ ___ ___ ___ ___ ___ ___ ___ ___ City of ___ ___ ___ ___ ___, State of ___ ___ ___ ___ ___ ___ ___ [Premises] to Tenant.

[LEASE TERM]

The Lease will start on ___ of ___ ___ ___, 20 ___ and will continue as a month-to-month tenancy. To terminate tenancy, the Landlord or Tenant must give the other party a ___ ___ day written notice of lease non-renewal.

[LEASE PAYMENTS]

The Tenant agrees to pay Landlord for the use of the Premises in the amount of $ ___ __, payable in advance on the first day of each month, except when day falls on a legal holiday or weekend, in which case rent is due on the next business day. Rent will be paid to Landlord at Landlord's address provided herein (or to other places as directed by Landlord) by mail to ___ ___ ___ ___ ___ ___ ___ ___ ___ ___ _ __ ___ or in person, at ___ ___ ___ ___ ___ ___ ___ ___ ___ ___ ___ ___ ___ ___ __.
Landlord will accept check made payable to ____________________________________
_or cashier's check made payable to ____
__or payment by ____________________________ to_____________________________

[LATE FEE]

Rent paid after the ___ ___ day of each month will be considered as late; and if rent is not paid within ___ ___ days of such due date, Tenant agrees to pay a late fee of ___ ___ ___ per day for every day that the rent is late.

[INSUFFICIENT FUNDS]

Tenant agrees to pay a charge of ___ ___ ___ for each check given by Tenant to Landlord that is returned to landlord for lack of sufficient funds.

[SECURITY DEPOSIT]

Upon execution of this Lease, Tenant shall deposit the sum of _____________to be held by the Landlord as security deposit for reasonable repair of damages to, or cleaning of the Premises upon the expiration or termination of this Lease, or other notable damages.

[USE OF PREMISES]

1. Tenant agrees that the Premises shall be used and occupied for no other purpose than as dwelling and that the Premises shall be occupied only by Tenant and the following named adults _____________

____

_____________________________ and the following named children _______________

____

__________ and no other without first obtaining a written consent from the Landlord.

2. The tenant hereby agrees to be responsible for the following utilities and or services ___ ___ ___ _

__ ___ ___ ___ ___ ___ ___ ___ ___ ___ ___ ___ ___ ___ ___ ________________

3. The Tenant is responsible for the following maintenance and or repairs ___ ___ ___ ___ ___ __

_ ___ ___ ___ ___ ___ ___ ___ ___ ___ ___ ___ ___ ___ _____ ___ ___ ___ ___

4. The tenant agrees not to keep any pets on the premises without priorly obtaining a written consent from the Landlord.

[ABANDONMENT AND RIGHT TO ENTER]

In any case that the Tenant abandons the Premises during the term of this Agreement, the Landlord has the right to enter the Premises by any means necessary without facing any liability and the Landlord may terminate this Agreement.

[AMENDMENTS]

The Landlord and Tenant agree that any amendments made to this Agreement must be in writing where they must be signed by both the Landlord and the Tenant. As such any amendment made by the parties will be applied to this Agreement.

[GOVERNING LAW]

This Agreement shall be governed by and construed in accordance with the laws of ___ ___ ___ ___

___ ___ ___ ___ ___ ___ ___ ___ ___ ___ ___ ___ ___ ____________________

TENANT

Name ____________________________

Signature _________________________

Date _____________________________

Witness ___________________________

Phone ____________________________

Address ___________________________

____

Signature _________________________

Date _____________________________

LANDLORD

Name ___________________________

Signature ________________________

Date ___________________________

Address _________________________

____

Witness _________________________

Phone __________________________

Address _________________________

Signature___________Date__________

MONTH-TO-MONTH RENTAL AGREEMENT

This lease agreement is made this __________ by and (between/among) _______ ___ ___ ___ ___ ___ ___ [Landlord] and ___ ___ ___ ___ ___ ___, [and other Tenants,] collectively [Tenant]. Each Tenant is jointly and severally liable for the payment of rent to the landlord and performance of all other terms in this Agreement.

[PREMISES]

Landlord hereby leases the premises located at ___ ___ ___ ___ ___ ___ ___ ___ ___ ___ City of ___ ___ ___ ___ ___, State of ___ ___ ___ ___ ___ ___ ___ ___ [Premises] to Tenant.

[LEASE TERM]

The Lease will start on ___ of ___ ___ ___, 20 ___ and will continue as a month-to-month tenancy. To terminate tenancy, the Landlord or Tenant must give the other party a ___ ___ day written notice of lease non-renewal.

[LEASE PAYMENTS]

The Tenant agrees to pay Landlord for the use of the Premises in the amount of $ ___ __, payable in advance on the first day of each month, except when day falls on a legal holiday or weekend, in which case rent is due on the next business day. Rent will be paid to Landlord at Landlord's address provided herein (or to other places as directed by Landlord) by mail to ___ ___ ___ ___ ___ ___ ___ ___ ___ ___ _ __ ___ or in person, at ___ ___ ___ ___ ___ ___ ___ ___ ___ ___ ___ ___ ___ ___ ___.

Landlord will accept check made payable to ______________________________

_or cashier's check made payable to ______________________________

__or payment by ___________________________ to___________________________

[LATE FEE]

Rent paid after the ___ ___ day of each month will be considered as late; and if rent is not paid within ___ ___ days of such due date, Tenant agrees to pay a late fee of ___ ___ ___ per day for every day that the rent is late.

[INSUFFICIENT FUNDS]

Tenant agrees to pay a charge of ___ ___ ___ for each check given by Tenant to Landlord that is returned to landlord for lack of sufficient funds.

[SECURITY DEPOSIT]

Upon execution of this Lease, Tenant shall deposit the sum of ____________to be held by the Landlord as security deposit for reasonable repair of damages to, or cleaning of the Premises upon the expiration or termination of this Lease, or other notable damages.

[USE OF PREMISES]

1. Tenant agrees that the Premises shall be used and occupied for no other purpose than as dwelling and that the Premises shall be occupied only by Tenant and the following named adults _____________

____

______________________________ and the following named children ______________

____

__________ and no other without first obtaining a written consent from the Landlord.

2. The tenant hereby agrees to be responsible for the following utilities and or services ___ ___ ___ _

__ ___ ___ ___ ___ ___ ___ ___ ___ ___ ___ ___ ___ ___ ________________

3. The Tenant is responsible for the following maintenance and or repairs ___ ___ ___ ___ ___ __

_ ___ ___ ___ ___ ___ ___ ___ ___ ___ ___ ___ ___ _____ ___ ___ ___

4. The tenant agrees not to keep any pets on the premises without priorly obtaining a written consent from the Landlord.

[ABANDONMENT AND RIGHT TO ENTER]

In any case that the Tenant abandons the Premises during the term of this Agreement, the Landlord has the right to enter the Premises by any means necessary without facing any liability and the Landlord may terminate this Agreement.

[AMENDMENTS]

The Landlord and Tenant agree that any amendments made to this Agreement must be in writing where they must be signed by both the Landlord and the Tenant. As such any amendment made by the parties will be applied to this Agreement.

[GOVERNING LAW]

This Agreement shall be governed by and construed in accordance with the laws of ___ ___ ___ ___

___ ___ ___ ___ ___ ___ ___ ___ ___ ___ ___ ___ ___ ___ __________________

TENANT

Name ______________________________

Signature ___________________________

Date _______________________________

Witness _____________________________

Phone ______________________________

Address _____________________________

____

Signature __________________________

Date ______________________________

LANDLORD

Name ____________________________

Signature _________________________

Date ___________________________ _

Address __________________________

____

Witness __________________________

Phone ____________________________

Address __________________________

Signature___________Date__________

MONTH-TO-MONTH RENTAL **AGREEMENT**

This lease agreement is made this __________ by and (between/among) _______ ___ ___ ___

___ ___ ___ [Landlord] and ___ ___ ___ ___ ___ ___ , [and other Tenants,] collectively [Tenant]. Each Tenant is jointly and severally liable for the payment of rent to the landlord and performance of all other terms in this Agreement.

[PREMISES]

Landlord hereby leases the premises located at ___ ___ ___ ___ ___ ___ ___ ___ ___ ___

City of ___ ___ ___ ___ ___, State of ___ ___ ___ ___ ___ ___ ___ ___ [Premises] to Tenant.

[LEASE TERM]

The Lease will start on ___ of ___ ___ ___, 20 ___ and will continue as a month-to-month tenancy. To terminate tenancy, the Landlord or Tenant must give the other party a ___ ___ day written notice of lease non-renewal.

[LEASE PAYMENTS]

The Tenant agrees to pay Landlord for the use of the Premises in the amount of $ ___ __, payable in advance on the first day of each month, except when day falls on a legal holiday or weekend, in which case rent is due on the next business day. Rent will be paid to Landlord at Landlord's address provided herein (or to other places as directed by Landlord) by mail to ___ ___ ___ ___ ___ ___ ___ ___ ___ ___ _

__ ___ or in person, at ___ ___ ___ ___ ___ ___ ___ ___ ___ ___ ___ ___ ___ __.

Landlord will accept check made payable to ______________________________

_or cashier's check made payable to _________________________________

__or payment by ___________________________ to_________________________

[LATE FEE]

Rent paid after the ___ ___ day of each month will be considered as late; and if rent is not paid within ___ ___ days of such due date, Tenant agrees to pay a late fee of ___ ___ ___ per day for every day that the rent is late.

[INSUFFICIENT FUNDS]

Tenant agrees to pay a charge of ___ ___ ___ for each check given by Tenant to Landlord that is returned to landlord for lack of sufficient funds.

[SECURITY DEPOSIT]

Upon execution of this Lease, Tenant shall deposit the sum of _____________to be held by the Landlord as security deposit for reasonable repair of damages to, or cleaning of the Premises upon the expiration or termination of this Lease, or other notable damages.

[USE OF PREMISES]

1. Tenant agrees that the Premises shall be used and occupied for no other purpose than as dwelling and that the Premises shall be occupied only by Tenant and the following named adults _____________

____

_____________________________ and the following named children _______________

____

__________ and no other without first obtaining a written consent from the Landlord.

2. The tenant hereby agrees to be responsible for the following utilities and or services ___ ___ ___ _

__ ___ ___ ___ ___ ___ ___ ___ ___ ___ ___ ___ ___ ___ ___________________

3. The Tenant is responsible for the following maintenance and or repairs ___ ___ ___ ___ ___ __

_ ___ ___ ___ ___ ___ ___ ___ ___ ___ ___ ___ ___ ___ _____ ___ ___ ___

4. The tenant agrees not to keep any pets on the premises without priorly obtaining a written consent from the Landlord.

[ABANDONMENT AND RIGHT TO ENTER]

In any case that the Tenant abandons the Premises during the term of this Agreement, the Landlord has the right to enter the Premises by any means necessary without facing any liability and the Landlord may terminate this Agreement.

[AMENDMENTS]

The Landlord and Tenant agree that any amendments made to this Agreement must be in writing where they must be signed by both the Landlord and the Tenant. As such any amendment made by the parties will be applied to this Agreement.

[GOVERNING LAW]

This Agreement shall be governed by and construed in accordance with the laws of ___ ___ ___ ___

___ ___ ___ ___ ___ ___ ___ ___ ___ ___ ___ ___ ___ ____________________

TENANT

Name ______________________________

Signature __________________________

Date _______________________________

Witness ____________________________

Phone ______________________________

Address ____________________________

____

Signature _________________________

Date ______________________________

LANDLORD

Name ______________________________

Signature __________________________

Date ______________________________

Address ____________________________

____

Witness ____________________________

Phone ______________________________

Address ____________________________

Signature____________Date__________

MONTH-TO-MONTH RENTAL **AGREEMENT**

This lease agreement is made this ___________ by and (between/among) _______ ___ ___ ___

___ ___ ___ [Landlord] and ___ ___ ___ ___ ___ ___ , [and other Tenants,] collectively [Tenant]. Each Tenant is jointly and severally liable for the payment of rent to the landlord and performance of all other terms in this Agreement.

[PREMISES]

Landlord hereby leases the premises located at ___ ___ ___ ___ ___ ___ ___ ___ ___ ___

City of ___ ___ ___ ___ ___, State of ___ ___ ___ ___ ___ ___ ___ ___ [Premises] to Tenant.

[LEASE TERM]

The Lease will start on ___ of ___ ___ ___, 20 ___ and will continue as a month-to-month tenancy. To terminate tenancy, the Landlord or Tenant must give the other party a ___ ___ day written notice of lease non-renewal.

[LEASE PAYMENTS]

The Tenant agrees to pay Landlord for the use of the Premises in the amount of $ ___ __, payable in advance on the first day of each month, except when day falls on a legal holiday or weekend, in which case rent is due on the next business day. Rent will be paid to Landlord at Landlord's address provided herein (or to other places as directed by Landlord) by mail to ___ ___ ___ ___ ___ ___ ___ ___ ___ ___ _

__ ___or in person, at ___ ___ ___ ___ ___ ___ ___ ___ ___ ___ ___ ___ ___ __.

Landlord will accept check made payable to ______________________________________

_or cashier's check made payable to ____

__or payment by ___________________________ to___________________________

[LATE FEE]

Rent paid after the ___ ___ day of each month will be considered as late; and if rent is not paid within ___ ___ days of such due date, Tenant agrees to pay a late fee of ___ ___ ___ per day for every day that the rent is late.

[INSUFFICIENT FUNDS]

Tenant agrees to pay a charge of ___ ___ ___ for each check given by Tenant to Landlord that is returned to landlord for lack of sufficient funds.

[SECURITY DEPOSIT]

Upon execution of this Lease, Tenant shall deposit the sum of _____________to be held by the Landlord as security deposit for reasonable repair of damages to, or cleaning of the Premises upon the expiration or termination of this Lease, or other notable damages.

[USE OF PREMISES]

1. Tenant agrees that the Premises shall be used and occupied for no other purpose than as dwelling and that the Premises shall be occupied only by Tenant and the following named adults _____________

____

_____________________________ and the following named children _______________

____

__________ and no other without first obtaining a written consent from the Landlord.

2. The tenant hereby agrees to be responsible for the following utilities and or services ___ ___ ___ _

__ ___ ___ ___ ___ ___ ___ ___ ___ ___ ___ ___ ___ ___ ___ _________________

3. The Tenant is responsible for the following maintenance and or repairs ___ ___ ___ ___ ___ __

_ ___ ___ ___ ___ ___ ___ ___ ___ ___ ___ ___ ___ ___ _____ ___ ___ ___ ___

4. The tenant agrees not to keep any pets on the premises without priorly obtaining a written consent from the Landlord.

[ABANDONMENT AND RIGHT TO ENTER]

In any case that the Tenant abandons the Premises during the term of this Agreement, the Landlord has the right to enter the Premises by any means necessary without facing any liability and the Landlord may terminate this Agreement.

[AMENDMENTS]

The Landlord and Tenant agree that any amendments made to this Agreement must be in writing where they must be signed by both the Landlord and the Tenant. As such any amendment made by the parties will be applied to this Agreement.

[GOVERNING LAW]

This Agreement shall be governed by and construed in accordance with the laws of ___ ___ ___ ___

___ ___ ___ ___ ___ ___ ___ ___ ___ ___ ___ ___ ___ ___ ___ ___________________

TENANT

Name ____________________________

Signature _________________________

Date _____________________________

Witness ___________________________

Phone ____________________________

Address ___________________________

____

Signature _________________________

Date _____________________________

LANDLORD

Name ____________________________

Signature _________________________

Date ____________________________ _

Address ___________________________

____

Witness ___________________________

Phone ____________________________

Address ___________________________

Signature___________Date__________

MONTH-TO-MONTH RENTAL AGREEMENT

This lease agreement is made this __________ by and (between/among) ______ ___ ___ ___ ___ ___ ___ [Landlord] and ___ ___ ___ ___ ___ ___, [and other Tenants,] collectively [Tenant]. Each Tenant is jointly and severally liable for the payment of rent to the landlord and performance of all other terms in this Agreement.

[PREMISES]

Landlord hereby leases the premises located at ___ ___ ___ ___ ___ ___ ___ ___ ___ ___ City of ___ ___ ___ ___ ___, State of ___ ___ ___ ___ ___ ___ ___ ___ [Premises] to Tenant.

[LEASE TERM]

The Lease will start on ___ of ___ ___ ___, 20 ___ and will continue as a month-to-month tenancy. To terminate tenancy, the Landlord or Tenant must give the other party a ___ ___ day written notice of lease non-renewal.

[LEASE PAYMENTS]

The Tenant agrees to pay Landlord for the use of the Premises in the amount of $ ___ __, payable in advance on the first day of each month, except when day falls on a legal holiday or weekend, in which case rent is due on the next business day. Rent will be paid to Landlord at Landlord's address provided herein (or to other places as directed by Landlord) by mail to ___ ___ ___ ___ ___ ___ ___ ___ ___ ___ _ __ ___ or in person, at ___ ___ ___ ___ ___ ___ ___ ___ ___ ___ ___ ___ ___ ___ __.
Landlord will accept check made payable to ___________________________________ _or cashier's check made payable to ______________________________________ __or payment by ___________________________ to___________________________

[LATE FEE]

Rent paid after the ___ ___ day of each month will be considered as late; and if rent is not paid within ___ ___ days of such due date, Tenant agrees to pay a late fee of ___ ___ ___ per day for every day that the rent is late.

[INSUFFICIENT FUNDS]

Tenant agrees to pay a charge of ___ ___ ___ for each check given by Tenant to Landlord that is returned to landlord for lack of sufficient funds.

[SECURITY DEPOSIT]

Upon execution of this Lease, Tenant shall deposit the sum of _____________to be held by the Landlord as security deposit for reasonable repair of damages to, or cleaning of the Premises upon the expiration or termination of this Lease, or other notable damages.

[USE OF PREMISES]

1. Tenant agrees that the Premises shall be used and occupied for no other purpose than as dwelling and that the Premises shall be occupied only by Tenant and the following named adults _____________

____

______________________________ and the following named children _______________

____

__________ and no other without first obtaining a written consent from the Landlord.

2. The tenant hereby agrees to be responsible for the following utilities and or services ___ ___ ___ _

__ ___ ___ ___ ___ ___ ___ ___ ___ ___ ___ ___ ___ ___ _________________

3. The Tenant is responsible for the following maintenance and or repairs ___ ___ ___ ___ ___ __

_ ___ ___ ___ ___ ___ ___ ___ ___ ___ ___ ___ ___ ___ ____ ___ ___ ___ ___

4. The tenant agrees not to keep any pets on the premises without priorly obtaining a written consent from the Landlord.

[ABANDONMENT AND RIGHT TO ENTER]

In any case that the Tenant abandons the Premises during the term of this Agreement, the Landlord has the right to enter the Premises by any means necessary without facing any liability and the Landlord may terminate this Agreement.

[AMENDMENTS]

The Landlord and Tenant agree that any amendments made to this Agreement must be in writing where they must be signed by both the Landlord and the Tenant. As such any amendment made by the parties will be applied to this Agreement.

[GOVERNING LAW]

This Agreement shall be governed by and construed in accordance with the laws of ___ ___ ___ ___

___ ___ ___ ___ ___ ___ ___ ___ ___ ___ ___ ___ ___ ___ ___ ___ ___ ___________________

TENANT

Name ____________________________

Signature __________________________

Date _____________________________

Witness ___________________________

Phone ____________________________

Address ___________________________

____

Signature _________________________

Date ____________________________

LANDLORD

Name ___________________________

Signature ________________________

Date __________________________ _

Address _________________________

____

Witness _________________________

Phone ___________________________

Address _________________________

Signature____________Date__________

MONTH-TO-MONTH RENTAL AGREEMENT

This lease agreement is made this __________ by and (between/among) _______ ___ ___ ___

___ ___ ___ [Landlord] and ___ ___ ___ ___ ___ ___, [and other Tenants,] collectively [Tenant]. Each Tenant is jointly and severally liable for the payment of rent to the landlord and performance of all other terms in this Agreement.

[PREMISES]

Landlord hereby leases the premises located at ___ ___ ___ ___ ___ ___ ___ ___ ___ ___

City of ___ ___ ___ ___ ___, State of ___ ___ ___ ___ ___ ___ ___ ___ [Premises] to Tenant.

[LEASE TERM]

The Lease will start on ___ of ___ ___ ___, 20 ___ and will continue as a month-to-month tenancy. To terminate tenancy, the Landlord or Tenant must give the other party a ___ ___ day written notice of lease non-renewal.

[LEASE PAYMENTS]

The Tenant agrees to pay Landlord for the use of the Premises in the amount of $ ___ __, payable in advance on the first day of each month, except when day falls on a legal holiday or weekend, in which case rent is due on the next business day. Rent will be paid to Landlord at Landlord's address provided herein (or to other places as directed by Landlord) by mail to ___ ___ ___ ___ ___ ___ ___ ___ ___ ___ _

__ ___ or in person, at ___ ___ ___ ___ ___ ___ ___ ___ ___ ___ ___ ___ ___ ___.

Landlord will accept check made payable to ______________________________

_or cashier's check made payable to ________________________________

__or payment by ___________________________ to___________________________

[LATE FEE]

Rent paid after the ___ ___ day of each month will be considered as late; and if rent is not paid within ___ ___ days of such due date, Tenant agrees to pay a late fee of ___ ___ ___ per day for every day that the rent is late.

[INSUFFICIENT FUNDS]

Tenant agrees to pay a charge of ___ ___ ___ for each check given by Tenant to Landlord that is returned to landlord for lack of sufficient funds.

[SECURITY DEPOSIT]

Upon execution of this Lease, Tenant shall deposit the sum of _____________to be held by the Landlord as security deposit for reasonable repair of damages to, or cleaning of the Premises upon the expiration or termination of this Lease, or other notable damages.

[USE OF PREMISES]

1. Tenant agrees that the Premises shall be used and occupied for no other purpose than as dwelling and that the Premises shall be occupied only by Tenant and the following named adults ______________

____

_______________________________ and the following named children ________________

____

__________ and no other without first obtaining a written consent from the Landlord.

2. The tenant hereby agrees to be responsible for the following utilities and or services ___ ___ ___ _

__ ___ ___ ___ ___ ___ ___ ___ ___ ___ ___ ___ ___ ___ __________________

3. The Tenant is responsible for the following maintenance and or repairs ___ ___ ___ ___ ___ __

_ ___ ___ ___ ___ ___ ___ ___ ___ ___ ___ ___ ___ _____ ___ ___ ___ ___

4. The tenant agrees not to keep any pets on the premises without priorly obtaining a written consent from the Landlord.

[ABANDONMENT AND RIGHT TO ENTER]

In any case that the Tenant abandons the Premises during the term of this Agreement, the Landlord has the right to enter the Premises by any means necessary without facing any liability and the Landlord may terminate this Agreement.

[AMENDMENTS]

The Landlord and Tenant agree that any amendments made to this Agreement must be in writing where they must be signed by both the Landlord and the Tenant. As such any amendment made by the parties will be applied to this Agreement.

[GOVERNING LAW]

This Agreement shall be governed by and construed in accordance with the laws of ___ ___ ___ ___

___ ___ ___ ___ ___ ___ ___ ___ ___ ___ ___ ___ ___ ____________________

TENANT

Name ______________________________

Signature ___________________________

Date _______________________________

Witness _____________________________

Phone ______________________________

Address _____________________________

____

Signature ___________________________

Date ______________________________

LANDLORD

Name ______________________________

Signature ___________________________

Date ____________________________ _

Address _____________________________

____

Witness _____________________________

Phone ______________________________

Address _____________________________

Signature____________Date__________

MONTH-TO-MONTH RENTAL **AGREEMENT**

This lease agreement is made this __________ by and (between/among) _______ ___ ___ ___ ___ ___ ___ [Landlord] and ___ ___ ___ ___ ___ ___, [and other Tenants,] collectively [Tenant]. Each Tenant is jointly and severally liable for the payment of rent to the landlord and performance of all other terms in this Agreement.

[PREMISES]

Landlord hereby leases the premises located at ___ ___ ___ ___ ___ ___ ___ ___ ___ ___ City of ___ ___ ___ ___ ___, State of ___ ___ ___ ___ ___ ___ ___ ___ ___ [Premises] to Tenant.

[LEASE TERM]

The Lease will start on ___ of ___ ___ ___, 20 ___ and will continue as a month-to-month tenancy. To terminate tenancy, the Landlord or Tenant must give the other party a ___ ___ day written notice of lease non-renewal.

[LEASE PAYMENTS]

The Tenant agrees to pay Landlord for the use of the Premises in the amount of $ ___ __, payable in advance on the first day of each month, except when day falls on a legal holiday or weekend, in which case rent is due on the next business day. Rent will be paid to Landlord at Landlord's address provided herein (or to other places as directed by Landlord) by mail to ___ ___ ___ ___ ___ ___ ___ ___ ___ ___ _ __ ___ or in person, at ___ ___ ___ ___ ___ ___ ___ ___ ___ ___ ___ ___ ___ ___ __.

Landlord will accept check made payable to ______________________________ _or cashier's check made payable to ______________________________ __or payment by __________________________ to____________________

[LATE FEE]

Rent paid after the ___ ___ day of each month will be considered as late; and if rent is not paid within ___ ___ days of such due date, Tenant agrees to pay a late fee of ___ ___ ___ per day for every day that the rent is late.

[INSUFFICIENT FUNDS]

Tenant agrees to pay a charge of ___ ___ ___ for each check given by Tenant to Landlord that is returned to landlord for lack of sufficient funds.

[SECURITY DEPOSIT]

Upon execution of this Lease, Tenant shall deposit the sum of ____________to be held by the Landlord as security deposit for reasonable repair of damages to, or cleaning of the Premises upon the expiration or termination of this Lease, or other notable damages.

[USE OF PREMISES]

1. Tenant agrees that the Premises shall be used and occupied for no other purpose than as dwelling and that the Premises shall be occupied only by Tenant and the following named adults _____________

____

______________________________ and the following named children _______________

____

__________ and no other without first obtaining a written consent from the Landlord.

2. The tenant hereby agrees to be responsible for the following utilities and or services ___ ___ ___ _

__ ___ ___ ___ ___ ___ ___ ___ ___ ___ ___ ___ ___ ___ ___________________

3. The Tenant is responsible for the following maintenance and or repairs ___ ___ ___ ___ ___ ___ __

_ ___ ___ ___ ___ ___ ___ ___ ___ ___ ___ ___ ___ ___ ___ ____ ___ ___ ___ ___

4. The tenant agrees not to keep any pets on the premises without priorly obtaining a written consent from the Landlord.

[ABANDONMENT AND RIGHT TO ENTER]

In any case that the Tenant abandons the Premises during the term of this Agreement, the Landlord has the right to enter the Premises by any means necessary without facing any liability and the Landlord may terminate this Agreement.

[AMENDMENTS]

The Landlord and Tenant agree that any amendments made to this Agreement must be in writing where they must be signed by both the Landlord and the Tenant. As such any amendment made by the parties will be applied to this Agreement.

[GOVERNING LAW]

This Agreement shall be governed by and construed in accordance with the laws of ___ ___ ___ ___

___ ___ ___ ___ ___ ___ ___ ___ ___ ___ ___ ___ ___ ___ ___ ___________________

TENANT

Name ____________________________

Signature _________________________

Date _____________________________

Witness ___________________________

Phone ____________________________

Address ___________________________

____

Signature _________________________

Date _____________________________

LANDLORD

Name ____________________________

Signature _________________________

Date ____________________________ _

Address ___________________________

____

Witness ___________________________

Phone ____________________________

Address ___________________________

Signature___________Date___________

MONTH-TO-MONTH RENTAL AGREEMENT

This lease agreement is made this __________ by and (between/among) _______ ___ ___ ___

___ ___ ___ [Landlord] and ___ ___ ___ ___ ___ ___, [and other Tenants,] collectively [Tenant]. Each Tenant is jointly and severally liable for the payment of rent to the landlord and performance of all other terms in this Agreement.

[PREMISES]

Landlord hereby leases the premises located at ___ ___ ___ ___ ___ ___ ___ ___ ___ ___

City of ___ ___ ___ ___ ___, State of ___ ___ ___ ___ ___ ___ ___ ___ [Premises] to Tenant.

[LEASE TERM]

The Lease will start on ___ of ___ ___ ___, 20 ___ and will continue as a month-to-month tenancy. To terminate tenancy, the Landlord or Tenant must give the other party a ___ ___ day written notice of lease non-renewal.

[LEASE PAYMENTS]

The Tenant agrees to pay Landlord for the use of the Premises in the amount of $ ___ __, payable in advance on the first day of each month, except when day falls on a legal holiday or weekend, in which case rent is due on the next business day. Rent will be paid to Landlord at Landlord's address provided herein (or to other places as directed by Landlord) by mail to ___ ___ ___ ___ ___ ___ ___ ___ ___ ___ _

__ ___ or in person, at ___ ___ ___ ___ ___ ___ ___ ___ ___ ___ ___ ___ ___ ___ __.

Landlord will accept check made payable to ____________________________

_or cashier's check made payable to ______________________________

__or payment by ___________________________ to____________________

[LATE FEE]

Rent paid after the ___ ___ day of each month will be considered as late; and if rent is not paid within ___ ___ days of such due date, Tenant agrees to pay a late fee of ___ ___ ___ per day for every day that the rent is late.

[INSUFFICIENT FUNDS]

Tenant agrees to pay a charge of ___ ___ ___ for each check given by Tenant to Landlord that is returned to landlord for lack of sufficient funds.

[SECURITY DEPOSIT]

Upon execution of this Lease, Tenant shall deposit the sum of ____________to be held by the Landlord as security deposit for reasonable repair of damages to, or cleaning of the Premises upon the expiration or termination of this Lease, or other notable damages.

[USE OF PREMISES]

1. Tenant agrees that the Premises shall be used and occupied for no other purpose than as dwelling and that the Premises shall be occupied only by Tenant and the following named adults _____________

____

_____________________________ and the following named children _______________

____

__________ and no other without first obtaining a written consent from the Landlord.

2. The tenant hereby agrees to be responsible for the following utilities and or services ___ ___ ___ _

__ ___ ___ ___ ___ ___ ___ ___ ___ ___ ___ ___ ___ ___ ___ ___ ________________

3. The Tenant is responsible for the following maintenance and or repairs ___ ___ ___ ___ ___ __

_ ___ ___ ___ ___ ___ ___ ___ ___ ___ ___ ___ ___ ___ _____ ___ ___ ___ ___

4. The tenant agrees not to keep any pets on the premises without priorly obtaining a written consent from the Landlord.

[ABANDONMENT AND RIGHT TO ENTER]

In any case that the Tenant abandons the Premises during the term of this Agreement, the Landlord has the right to enter the Premises by any means necessary without facing any liability and the Landlord may terminate this Agreement.

[AMENDMENTS]

The Landlord and Tenant agree that any amendments made to this Agreement must be in writing where they must be signed by both the Landlord and the Tenant. As such any amendment made by the parties will be applied to this Agreement.

[GOVERNING LAW]

This Agreement shall be governed by and construed in accordance with the laws of ___ ___ ___ ___

___ ___ ___ ___ ___ ___ ___ ___ ___ ___ ___ _______________________

TENANT

Name ____________________________

Signature __________________________

Date _____________________________

Witness ___________________________

Phone ____________________________

Address ___________________________

____

Signature _________________________

Date ____________________________

LANDLORD

Name ___________________________

Signature ________________________

Date ____________________________ _

Address __________________________

____

Witness __________________________

Phone ___________________________

Address __________________________

Signature____________Date__________

MONTH-TO-MONTH RENTAL AGREEMENT

This lease agreement is made this __________ by and (between/among) _______ ___ ___ ___ ___ ___ ___ [Landlord] and ___ ___ ___ ___ ___ ___ , [and other Tenants,] collectively [Tenant]. Each Tenant is jointly and severally liable for the payment of rent to the landlord and performance of all other terms in this Agreement.

[PREMISES]

Landlord hereby leases the premises located at ___ ___ ___ ___ ___ ___ ___ ___ ___ ___

City of ___ ___ ___ ___ ___, State of ___ ___ ___ ___ ___ ___ ___ [Premises] to Tenant.

[LEASE TERM]

The Lease will start on ___ of ___ ___ ___, 20 ___ and will continue as a month-to-month tenancy. To terminate tenancy, the Landlord or Tenant must give the other party a ___ ___ day written notice of lease non-renewal.

[LEASE PAYMENTS]

The Tenant agrees to pay Landlord for the use of the Premises in the amount of $ ___ __, payable in advance on the first day of each month, except when day falls on a legal holiday or weekend, in which case rent is due on the next business day. Rent will be paid to Landlord at Landlord's address provided herein (or to other places as directed by Landlord) by mail to ___ ___ ___ ___ ___ ___ ___ ___ ___ ___ _ __ ___ or in person, at ___ ___ ___ ___ ___ ___ ___ ___ ___ ___ ___ ___ ___ ___ __.

Landlord will accept check made payable to ______________________________

_or cashier's check made payable to ______________________________

__or payment by __________________________ to__________________________

[LATE FEE]

Rent paid after the ___ ___ day of each month will be considered as late; and if rent is not paid within ___ ___ days of such due date, Tenant agrees to pay a late fee of ___ ___ ___ per day for every day that the rent is late.

[INSUFFICIENT FUNDS]

Tenant agrees to pay a charge of ___ ___ ___ for each check given by Tenant to Landlord that is returned to landlord for lack of sufficient funds.

[SECURITY DEPOSIT]

Upon execution of this Lease, Tenant shall deposit the sum of _____________to be held by the Landlord as security deposit for reasonable repair of damages to, or cleaning of the Premises upon the expiration or termination of this Lease, or other notable damages.

[USE OF PREMISES]

1. Tenant agrees that the Premises shall be used and occupied for no other purpose than as dwelling and that the Premises shall be occupied only by Tenant and the following named adults _____________

____

_______________________________ and the following named children ______________

____

__________ and no other without first obtaining a written consent from the Landlord.

2. The tenant hereby agrees to be responsible for the following utilities and or services ___ ___ ___ _

__ ___ ___ ___ ___ ___ ___ ___ ___ ___ ___ ___ ___ ___ ___________________

3. The Tenant is responsible for the following maintenance and or repairs ___ ___ ___ ___ ___ __

_ ___ ___ ___ ___ ___ ___ ___ ___ ___ ___ ___ ___ ___ ____ ___ ___ ___ ___

4. The tenant agrees not to keep any pets on the premises without priorly obtaining a written consent from the Landlord.

[ABANDONMENT AND RIGHT TO ENTER]

In any case that the Tenant abandons the Premises during the term of this Agreement, the Landlord has the right to enter the Premises by any means necessary without facing any liability and the Landlord may terminate this Agreement.

[AMENDMENTS]

The Landlord and Tenant agree that any amendments made to this Agreement must be in writing where they must be signed by both the Landlord and the Tenant. As such any amendment made by the parties will be applied to this Agreement.

[GOVERNING LAW]

This Agreement shall be governed by and construed in accordance with the laws of ___ ___ ___ ___

___ ___ ___ ___ ___ ___ ___ ___ ___ ___ ___ ___ ___ ___________________

TENANT

Name ______________________________

Signature ___________________________

Date _______________________________

Witness _____________________________

Phone ______________________________

Address _____________________________

____

Signature ___________________________

Date ______________________________

LANDLORD

Name ____________________________

Signature __________________________

Date ____________________________ _

Address __________________________

____

Witness __________________________

Phone ____________________________

Address __________________________

Signature___________Date__________

MONTH-TO-MONTH RENTAL **AGREEMENT**

This lease agreement is made this __________ by and (between/among) _______ ___ ___ ___ ___ ___ ___ [Landlord] and ___ ___ ___ ___ ___ ___, [and other Tenants,] collectively [Tenant]. Each Tenant is jointly and severally liable for the payment of rent to the landlord and performance of all other terms in this Agreement.

[PREMISES]

Landlord hereby leases the premises located at ___ ___ ___ ___ ___ ___ ___ ___ ___ ___ ___ City of ___ ___ ___ ___ ___, State of ___ ___ ___ ___ ___ ___ ___ [Premises] to Tenant.

[LEASE TERM]

The Lease will start on ___ of ___ ___ ___, 20 ___ and will continue as a month-to-month tenancy. To terminate tenancy, the Landlord or Tenant must give the other party a ___ ___ day written notice of lease non-renewal.

[LEASE PAYMENTS]

The Tenant agrees to pay Landlord for the use of the Premises in the amount of $ ___ __, payable in advance on the first day of each month, except when day falls on a legal holiday or weekend, in which case rent is due on the next business day. Rent will be paid to Landlord at Landlord's address provided herein (or to other places as directed by Landlord) by mail to ___ ___ ___ ___ ___ ___ ___ ___ ___ ___ _ __ ___ or in person, at ___ ___ ___ ___ ___ ___ ___ ___ ___ ___ ___ ___ ___ ___ __. Landlord will accept check made payable to _________________________________ _or cashier's check made payable to _________________________________ __or payment by ___________________________ to___________________________

[LATE FEE]

Rent paid after the ___ ___ day of each month will be considered as late; and if rent is not paid within ___ ___ days of such due date, Tenant agrees to pay a late fee of ___ ___ ___ per day for every day that the rent is late.

[INSUFFICIENT FUNDS]

Tenant agrees to pay a charge of ___ ___ ___ for each check given by Tenant to Landlord that is returned to landlord for lack of sufficient funds.

[SECURITY DEPOSIT]

Upon execution of this Lease, Tenant shall deposit the sum of _____________to be held by the Landlord as security deposit for reasonable repair of damages to, or cleaning of the Premises upon the expiration or termination of this Lease, or other notable damages.

[USE OF PREMISES]

1. Tenant agrees that the Premises shall be used and occupied for no other purpose than as dwelling and that the Premises shall be occupied only by Tenant and the following named adults _____________

____

______________________________ and the following named children _______________

____

__________ and no other without first obtaining a written consent from the Landlord.

2. The tenant hereby agrees to be responsible for the following utilities and or services ___ ___ ___ _

__ ___ ___ ___ ___ ___ ___ ___ ___ ___ ___ ___ ___ ___ ________________

3. The Tenant is responsible for the following maintenance and or repairs ___ ___ ___ ___ ___ __

_ ___ ___ ___ ___ ___ ___ ___ ___ ___ ___ ___ ___ _____ ___ ___ ___ ___

4. The tenant agrees not to keep any pets on the premises without priorly obtaining a written consent from the Landlord.

[ABANDONMENT AND RIGHT TO ENTER]

In any case that the Tenant abandons the Premises during the term of this Agreement, the Landlord has the right to enter the Premises by any means necessary without facing any liability and the Landlord may terminate this Agreement.

[AMENDMENTS]

The Landlord and Tenant agree that any amendments made to this Agreement must be in writing where they must be signed by both the Landlord and the Tenant. As such any amendment made by the parties will be applied to this Agreement.

[GOVERNING LAW]

This Agreement shall be governed by and construed in accordance with the laws of ___ ___ ___ ___

___ ___ ___ ___ ___ ___ ___ ___ ___ ___ ___ ___ ___ ___ ___________________

TENANT

Name ____________________________

Signature __________________________

Date _____________________________

Witness ___________________________

Phone ____________________________

Address ___________________________

____

Signature __________________________

Date _____________________________

LANDLORD

Name ____________________________

Signature __________________________

Date ___________________________ _

Address __________________________

____

Witness __________________________

Phone ___________________________

Address __________________________

Signature____________Date__________

MONTH-TO-MONTH RENTAL **AGREEMENT**

This lease agreement is made this _ _ _ _ _ _ _ __ _ _ by and (between/among) _ [Landlord] and _ , [and other Tenants,] collectively [Tenant]. Each Tenant is jointly and severally liable for the payment of rent to the landlord and performance of all other terms in this Agreement.

[PREMISES]

Landlord hereby leases the premises located at _ City of _ _ _ _ _ _ _ _ _ _ _ _ _ _ _ , State of _ [Premises] to Tenant.

[LEASE TERM]

The Lease will start on _ _ _ of _ _ _ _ _ _ _ _ _ , 20 _ _ _ and will continue as a month-to-month tenancy. To terminate tenancy, the Landlord or Tenant must give the other party a _ _ _ _ _ _ day written notice of lease non-renewal.

[LEASE PAYMENTS]

The Tenant agrees to pay Landlord for the use of the Premises in the amount of $ _ _ _ _ _, payable in advance on the first day of each month, except when day falls on a legal holiday or weekend, in which case rent is due on the next business day. Rent will be paid to Landlord at Landlord's address provided herein (or to other places as directed by Landlord) by mail to _ or in person, at _ .
Landlord will accept check made payable to _or cashier's check made payable to _or payment by _ to_ _

[LATE FEE]

Rent paid after the _ _ _ _ _ _ day of each month will be considered as late; and if rent is not paid within _ _ _ _ _ _ days of such due date, Tenant agrees to pay a late fee of _ _ _ _ _ _ _ _ _ per day for every day that the rent is late.

[INSUFFICIENT FUNDS]

Tenant agrees to pay a charge of _ _ _ _ _ _ _ _ _ for each check given by Tenant to Landlord that is returned to landlord for lack of sufficient funds.

[SECURITY DEPOSIT]

Upon execution of this Lease, Tenant shall deposit the sum of _ _ _ _ _ _ _ _ _ _ _ _ _to be held by the Landlord as security deposit for reasonable repair of damages to, or cleaning of the Premises upon the expiration or termination of this Lease, or other notable damages.

[USE OF PREMISES]

1. Tenant agrees that the Premises shall be used and occupied for no other purpose than as dwelling and that the Premises shall be occupied only by Tenant and the following named adults _____________

____

______________________________ and the following named children _______________

____

__________ and no other without first obtaining a written consent from the Landlord.

2. The tenant hereby agrees to be responsible for the following utilities and or services ___ ___ ___ _

__ ___ ___ ___ ___ ___ ___ ___ ___ ___ ___ ___ ___ ___________________

3. The Tenant is responsible for the following maintenance and or repairs ___ ___ ___ ___ ___ __

_ ___ ___ ___ ___ ___ ___ ___ ___ ___ ___ ___ ___ ___ _____ ___ ___ ___ ___

4. The tenant agrees not to keep any pets on the premises without priorly obtaining a written consent from the Landlord.

[ABANDONMENT AND RIGHT TO ENTER]

In any case that the Tenant abandons the Premises during the term of this Agreement, the Landlord has the right to enter the Premises by any means necessary without facing any liability and the Landlord may terminate this Agreement.

[AMENDMENTS]

The Landlord and Tenant agree that any amendments made to this Agreement must be in writing where they must be signed by both the Landlord and the Tenant. As such any amendment made by the parties will be applied to this Agreement.

[GOVERNING LAW]

This Agreement shall be governed by and construed in accordance with the laws of ___ ___ ___ ___

___ ___ ___ ___ ___ ___ ___ ___ ___ ___ ___ ___ ___ ___ ___ ___ ____________________

TENANT

Name ______________________________

Signature ___________________________

Date _______________________________

Witness _____________________________

Phone ______________________________

Address _____________________________

____

Signature __________________________

Date ______________________________

LANDLORD

Name _____________________________

Signature ___________________________

Date ______________________________

Address ____________________________

____

Witness ____________________________

Phone ______________________________

Address ____________________________

Signature___________Date___________

MONTH-TO-MONTH RENTAL **AGREEMENT**

This lease agreement is made this ___________ by and (between/among) _______ ___ ___ ___ ___ ___ ___ [Landlord] and ___ ___ ___ ___ ___ ___, [and other Tenants,] collectively [Tenant]. Each Tenant is jointly and severally liable for the payment of rent to the landlord and performance of all other terms in this Agreement.

[PREMISES]

Landlord hereby leases the premises located at ___ ___ ___ ___ ___ ___ ___ ___ ___ ___ City of ___ ___ ___ ___ ___, State of ___ ___ ___ ___ ___ ___ ___ [Premises] to Tenant.

[LEASE TERM]

The Lease will start on ___ of ___ ___ ___, 20 ___ and will continue as a month-to-month tenancy. To terminate tenancy, the Landlord or Tenant must give the other party a ___ ___ day written notice of lease non-renewal.

[LEASE PAYMENTS]

The Tenant agrees to pay Landlord for the use of the Premises in the amount of $ ___ __, payable in advance on the first day of each month, except when day falls on a legal holiday or weekend, in which case rent is due on the next business day. Rent will be paid to Landlord at Landlord's address provided herein (or to other places as directed by Landlord) by mail to ___ ___ ___ ___ ___ ___ ___ ___ ___ ___ _ __ ___ or in person, at ___ ___ ___ ___ ___ ___ ___ ___ ___ ___ ___ ___ ___ ___ __. Landlord will accept check made payable to _______________________________ _or cashier's check made payable to _______________________________ __or payment by ___________________________ to___________________________

[LATE FEE]

Rent paid after the ___ ___ day of each month will be considered as late; and if rent is not paid within ___ ___ days of such due date, Tenant agrees to pay a late fee of ___ ___ ___ per day for every day that the rent is late.

[INSUFFICIENT FUNDS]

Tenant agrees to pay a charge of ___ ___ ___ for each check given by Tenant to Landlord that is returned to landlord for lack of sufficient funds.

[SECURITY DEPOSIT]

Upon execution of this Lease, Tenant shall deposit the sum of ______________to be held by the Landlord as security deposit for reasonable repair of damages to, or cleaning of the Premises upon the expiration or termination of this Lease, or other notable damages.

[USE OF PREMISES]

1. Tenant agrees that the Premises shall be used and occupied for no other purpose than as dwelling and that the Premises shall be occupied only by Tenant and the following named adults _____________

____

_____________________________ and the following named children _______________

____

__________ and no other without first obtaining a written consent from the Landlord.

2. The tenant hereby agrees to be responsible for the following utilities and or services ___ ___ ___ _

__ ___ ___ ___ ___ ___ ___ ___ ___ ___ ___ ___ ___ ___ ___________________

3. The Tenant is responsible for the following maintenance and or repairs ___ ___ ___ ___ ___ __

_ ___ ___ ___ ___ ___ ___ ___ ___ ___ ___ ___ ___ ___ ____ ___ ___ ___

4. The tenant agrees not to keep any pets on the premises without priorly obtaining a written consent from the Landlord.

[ABANDONMENT AND RIGHT TO ENTER]

In any case that the Tenant abandons the Premises during the term of this Agreement, the Landlord has the right to enter the Premises by any means necessary without facing any liability and the Landlord may terminate this Agreement.

[AMENDMENTS]

The Landlord and Tenant agree that any amendments made to this Agreement must be in writing where they must be signed by both the Landlord and the Tenant. As such any amendment made by the parties will be applied to this Agreement.

[GOVERNING LAW]

This Agreement shall be governed by and construed in accordance with the laws of ___ ___ ___ ___

___ ___ ___ ___ ___ ___ ___ ___ ___ ___ ___ ___ ___ ___ ___________________

TENANT

Name ______________________________

Signature ___________________________

Date _______________________________

Witness _____________________________

Phone ______________________________

Address _____________________________

____

Signature __________________________

Date ______________________________

LANDLORD

Name ____________________________

Signature __________________________

Date _____________________________

Address ___________________________

____

Witness ___________________________

Phone _____________________________

Address ___________________________

Signature___________Date__________

MONTH-TO-MONTH RENTAL **AGREEMENT**

This lease agreement is made this __________ by and (between/among) _______ ___ ___ ___ ___ ___ ___ [Landlord] and ___ ___ ___ ___ ___ ___, [and other Tenants,] collectively [Tenant]. Each Tenant is jointly and severally liable for the payment of rent to the landlord and performance of all other terms in this Agreement.

[PREMISES]

Landlord hereby leases the premises located at ___ ___ ___ ___ ___ ___ ___ ___ ___ ___ City of ___ ___ ___ ___ ___, State of ___ ___ ___ ___ ___ ___ ___ [Premises] to Tenant.

[LEASE TERM]

The Lease will start on ___ of ___ ___ ___, 20 ___ and will continue as a month-to-month tenancy. To terminate tenancy, the Landlord or Tenant must give the other party a ___ ___ day written notice of lease non-renewal.

[LEASE PAYMENTS]

The Tenant agrees to pay Landlord for the use of the Premises in the amount of $ ___ __, payable in advance on the first day of each month, except when day falls on a legal holiday or weekend, in which case rent is due on the next business day. Rent will be paid to Landlord at Landlord's address provided herein (or to other places as directed by Landlord) by mail to ___ ___ ___ ___ ___ ___ ___ ___ ___ ___ _ __ ___ or in person, at ___ ___ ___ ___ ___ ___ ___ ___ ___ ___ ___ ___ ___ ___ __. Landlord will accept check made payable to ______________________________________ _or cashier's check made payable to ____ __or payment by ___________________________ to___________________________

[LATE FEE]

Rent paid after the ___ ___ day of each month will be considered as late; and if rent is not paid within ___ ___ days of such due date, Tenant agrees to pay a late fee of ___ ___ ___ per day for every day that the rent is late.

[INSUFFICIENT FUNDS]

Tenant agrees to pay a charge of ___ ___ ___ for each check given by Tenant to Landlord that is returned to landlord for lack of sufficient funds.

[SECURITY DEPOSIT]

Upon execution of this Lease, Tenant shall deposit the sum of _____________ to be held by the Landlord as security deposit for reasonable repair of damages to, or cleaning of the Premises upon the expiration or termination of this Lease, or other notable damages.

[USE OF PREMISES]

1. Tenant agrees that the Premises shall be used and occupied for no other purpose than as dwelling and that the Premises shall be occupied only by Tenant and the following named adults _____________

____

______________________________ and the following named children _______________

____

__________ and no other without first obtaining a written consent from the Landlord.

2. The tenant hereby agrees to be responsible for the following utilities and or services ___ ___ ___ _

__ ___ ___ ___ ___ ___ ___ ___ ___ ___ ___ ___ ___ ________________

3. The Tenant is responsible for the following maintenance and or repairs ___ ___ ___ ___ ___ __

_ ___ ___ ___ ___ ___ ___ ___ ___ ___ ___ ___ ___ ____ ___ ___ ___ ___

4. The tenant agrees not to keep any pets on the premises without priorly obtaining a written consent from the Landlord.

[ABANDONMENT AND RIGHT TO ENTER]

In any case that the Tenant abandons the Premises during the term of this Agreement, the Landlord has the right to enter the Premises by any means necessary without facing any liability and the Landlord may terminate this Agreement.

[AMENDMENTS]

The Landlord and Tenant agree that any amendments made to this Agreement must be in writing where they must be signed by both the Landlord and the Tenant. As such any amendment made by the parties will be applied to this Agreement.

[GOVERNING LAW]

This Agreement shall be governed by and construed in accordance with the laws of ___ ___ ___ ___

___ ___ ___ ___ ___ ___ ___ ___ ___ ___ ___ ___ ____________________

TENANT

Name ______________________________

Signature ___________________________

Date ________________________________

Witness _____________________________

Phone ______________________________

Address _____________________________

____

Signature ___________________________

Date ______________________________

LANDLORD

Name ______________________________

Signature ___________________________

Date ____________________________ _

Address _____________________________

____

Witness _____________________________

Phone ______________________________

Address _____________________________

Signature___________Date__________

MONTH-TO-MONTH RENTAL **AGREEMENT**

This lease agreement is made this __________ by and (between/among) ________ ___ ___ ___ ___ ___ ___ [Landlord] and ___ ___ ___ ___ ___ ___ , [and other Tenants,] collectively [Tenant]. Each Tenant is jointly and severally liable for the payment of rent to the landlord and performance of all other terms in this Agreement.

[PREMISES]

Landlord hereby leases the premises located at ___ ___ ___ ___ ___ ___ ___ ___ ___ ___

City of ___ ___ ___ ___ ___, State of ___ ___ ___ ___ ___ ___ ___ ___ [Premises] to Tenant.

[LEASE TERM]

The Lease will start on ___ of ___ ___ ___, 20 ___ and will continue as a month-to-month tenancy. To terminate tenancy, the Landlord or Tenant must give the other party a ___ ___ day written notice of lease non-renewal.

[LEASE PAYMENTS]

The Tenant agrees to pay Landlord for the use of the Premises in the amount of $ ___ __, payable in advance on the first day of each month, except when day falls on a legal holiday or weekend, in which case rent is due on the next business day. Rent will be paid to Landlord at Landlord's address provided herein (or to other places as directed by Landlord) by mail to ___ ___ ___ ___ ___ ___ ___ ___ ___ ___ _ __ ___ or in person, at ___ ___ ___ ___ ___ ___ ___ ___ ___ ___ ___ ___ ___ __.

Landlord will accept check made payable to ______________________________________

_or cashier's check made payable to ____

__or payment by __________________________ to__________________________

[LATE FEE]

Rent paid after the ___ ___ day of each month will be considered as late; and if rent is not paid within ___ ___ days of such due date, Tenant agrees to pay a late fee of ___ ___ ___ per day for every day that the rent is late.

[INSUFFICIENT FUNDS]

Tenant agrees to pay a charge of ___ ___ ___ for each check given by Tenant to Landlord that is returned to landlord for lack of sufficient funds.

[SECURITY DEPOSIT]

Upon execution of this Lease, Tenant shall deposit the sum of _____________to be held by the Landlord as security deposit for reasonable repair of damages to, or cleaning of the Premises upon the expiration or termination of this Lease, or other notable damages.

[USE OF PREMISES]

1. Tenant agrees that the Premises shall be used and occupied for no other purpose than as dwelling and that the Premises shall be occupied only by Tenant and the following named adults _____________

____

______________________________ and the following named children ______________

____

__________ and no other without first obtaining a written consent from the Landlord.

2. The tenant hereby agrees to be responsible for the following utilities and or services ___ ___ ___ _

__ ___ ___ ___ ___ ___ ___ ___ ___ ___ ___ ___ ___ ___ _________________

3. The Tenant is responsible for the following maintenance and or repairs ___ ___ ___ ___ ___ __

_ ___ ___ ___ ___ ___ ___ ___ ___ ___ ___ ___ ___ ___ _____ ___ ___ ___ ___

4. The tenant agrees not to keep any pets on the premises without priorly obtaining a written consent from the Landlord.

[ABANDONMENT AND RIGHT TO ENTER]

In any case that the Tenant abandons the Premises during the term of this Agreement, the Landlord has the right to enter the Premises by any means necessary without facing any liability and the Landlord may terminate this Agreement.

[AMENDMENTS]

The Landlord and Tenant agree that any amendments made to this Agreement must be in writing where they must be signed by both the Landlord and the Tenant. As such any amendment made by the parties will be applied to this Agreement.

[GOVERNING LAW]

This Agreement shall be governed by and construed in accordance with the laws of ___ ___ ___ ___

___ ___ ___ ___ ___ ___ ___ ___ ___ ___ ___ ___ ___ ___ ___________________

TENANT

Name ______________________________

Signature ___________________________

Date _______________________________

Witness ____________________________

Phone ______________________________

Address ____________________________

____

Signature __________________________

Date _______________________________

LANDLORD

Name ____________________________

Signature _________________________

Date ____________________________ _

Address ___________________________

____

Witness ___________________________

Phone _____________________________

Address ___________________________

Signature___________Date__________

MONTH-TO-MONTH RENTAL **AGREEMENT**

This lease agreement is made this __________ by and (between/among) _______ ___ ___ ___ ___ ___ ___ [Landlord] and ___ ___ ___ ___ ___ ___, [and other Tenants,] collectively [Tenant]. Each Tenant is jointly and severally liable for the payment of rent to the landlord and performance of all other terms in this Agreement.

[PREMISES]

Landlord hereby leases the premises located at ___ ___ ___ ___ ___ ___ ___ ___ ___ ___ City of ___ ___ ___ ___ ___, State of ___ ___ ___ ___ ___ ___ ___ [Premises] to Tenant.

[LEASE TERM]

The Lease will start on ___ of ___ ___ ___, 20 ___ and will continue as a month-to-month tenancy. To terminate tenancy, the Landlord or Tenant must give the other party a ___ ___ day written notice of lease non-renewal.

[LEASE PAYMENTS]

The Tenant agrees to pay Landlord for the use of the Premises in the amount of $ ___ __, payable in advance on the first day of each month, except when day falls on a legal holiday or weekend, in which case rent is due on the next business day. Rent will be paid to Landlord at Landlord's address provided herein (or to other places as directed by Landlord) by mail to ___ ___ ___ ___ ___ ___ ___ ___ ___ ___ _ __ ___ or in person, at ___ ___ ___ ___ ___ ___ ___ ___ ___ ___ ___ ___ ___ ___ __. Landlord will accept check made payable to _________________________________ _or cashier's check made payable to ___________________________________ __or payment by ___________________________ to____________________________

[LATE FEE]

Rent paid after the ___ ___ day of each month will be considered as late; and if rent is not paid within ___ ___ days of such due date, Tenant agrees to pay a late fee of ___ ___ ___ per day for every day that the rent is late.

[INSUFFICIENT FUNDS]

Tenant agrees to pay a charge of ___ ___ ___ for each check given by Tenant to Landlord that is returned to landlord for lack of sufficient funds.

[SECURITY DEPOSIT]

Upon execution of this Lease, Tenant shall deposit the sum of _____________to be held by the Landlord as security deposit for reasonable repair of damages to, or cleaning of the Premises upon the expiration or termination of this Lease, or other notable damages.

[USE OF PREMISES]

1. Tenant agrees that the Premises shall be used and occupied for no other purpose than as dwelling and that the Premises shall be occupied only by Tenant and the following named adults _____________ ____ _____________________________ and the following named children _______________ ____ __________ and no other without first obtaining a written consent from the Landlord.

2. The tenant hereby agrees to be responsible for the following utilities and or services ___ ___ ___ _ __ ___ ___ ___ ___ ___ ___ ___ ___ ___ ___ ___ _________________

3. The Tenant is responsible for the following maintenance and or repairs ___ ___ ___ ___ ___ __ _ ___ ___ ___ ___ ___ ___ ___ ___ ___ ___ ___ ___ _____ ___ ___ ___ ___

4. The tenant agrees not to keep any pets on the premises without priorly obtaining a written consent from the Landlord.

[ABANDONMENT AND RIGHT TO ENTER]

In any case that the Tenant abandons the Premises during the term of this Agreement, the Landlord has the right to enter the Premises by any means necessary without facing any liability and the Landlord may terminate this Agreement.

[AMENDMENTS]

The Landlord and Tenant agree that any amendments made to this Agreement must be in writing where they must be signed by both the Landlord and the Tenant. As such any amendment made by the parties will be applied to this Agreement.

[GOVERNING LAW]

This Agreement shall be governed by and construed in accordance with the laws of ___________________

TENANT

Name ____________________________

Signature ___________________________

Date _______________________________

Witness _____________________________

Phone ______________________________

Address _____________________________

____

Signature _________________________

Date ____________________________

LANDLORD

Name ____________________________

Signature _________________________

Date __________________________ _

Address ___________________________

____

Witness ___________________________

Phone ____________________________

Address ___________________________

Signature___________Date__________

MONTH-TO-MONTH RENTAL **AGREEMENT**

This lease agreement is made this __________ by and (between/among) _______ ___ ___ ___ ___ ___ ___ [Landlord] and ___ ___ ___ ___ ___ ___, [and other Tenants,] collectively [Tenant]. Each Tenant is jointly and severally liable for the payment of rent to the landlord and performance of all other terms in this Agreement.

[PREMISES]

Landlord hereby leases the premises located at ___ ___ ___ ___ ___ ___ ___ ___ ___ ___ City of ___ ___ ___ ___ ___, State of ___ ___ ___ ___ ___ ___ ___ [Premises] to Tenant.

[LEASE TERM]

The Lease will start on ___ of ___ ___ ___, 20 ___ and will continue as a month-to-month tenancy. To terminate tenancy, the Landlord or Tenant must give the other party a ___ ___ day written notice of lease non-renewal.

[LEASE PAYMENTS]

The Tenant agrees to pay Landlord for the use of the Premises in the amount of $ ___ __, payable in advance on the first day of each month, except when day falls on a legal holiday or weekend, in which case rent is due on the next business day. Rent will be paid to Landlord at Landlord's address provided herein (or to other places as directed by Landlord) by mail to ___ ___ ___ ___ ___ ___ ___ ___ ___ ___ _ __ ___ or in person, at ___ ___ ___ ___ ___ ___ ___ ___ ___ ___ ___ ___ ___ __. Landlord will accept check made payable to ______________________________________ _or cashier's check made payable to ____ __or payment by ___________________________ to_________________________

[LATE FEE]

Rent paid after the ___ ___ day of each month will be considered as late; and if rent is not paid within ___ ___ days of such due date, Tenant agrees to pay a late fee of ___ ___ ___ per day for every day that the rent is late.

[INSUFFICIENT FUNDS]

Tenant agrees to pay a charge of ___ ___ ___ for each check given by Tenant to Landlord that is returned to landlord for lack of sufficient funds.

[SECURITY DEPOSIT]

Upon execution of this Lease, Tenant shall deposit the sum of _____________to be held by the Landlord as security deposit for reasonable repair of damages to, or cleaning of the Premises upon the expiration or termination of this Lease, or other notable damages.

[USE OF PREMISES]

1. Tenant agrees that the Premises shall be used and occupied for no other purpose than as dwelling and that the Premises shall be occupied only by Tenant and the following named adults _____________ ____ _____________________________ and the following named children _______________ ____ __________ and no other without first obtaining a written consent from the Landlord.

2. The tenant hereby agrees to be responsible for the following utilities and or services ___ ___ ___ _ __ ___ ___ ___ ___ ___ ___ ___ ___ ___ ___ ___ ___ _________________

3. The Tenant is responsible for the following maintenance and or repairs ___ ___ ___ ___ ___ __ _ ___ ___ ___ ___ ___ ___ ___ ___ ___ ___ ___ ___ _____ ___ ___ ___ ___

4. The tenant agrees not to keep any pets on the premises without priorly obtaining a written consent from the Landlord.

[ABANDONMENT AND RIGHT TO ENTER]

In any case that the Tenant abandons the Premises during the term of this Agreement, the Landlord has the right to enter the Premises by any means necessary without facing any liability and the Landlord may terminate this Agreement.

[AMENDMENTS]

The Landlord and Tenant agree that any amendments made to this Agreement must be in writing where they must be signed by both the Landlord and the Tenant. As such any amendment made by the parties will be applied to this Agreement.

[GOVERNING LAW]

This Agreement shall be governed by and construed in accordance with the laws of ___________________

TENANT

Name ____________________________

Signature _________________________

Date _____________________________

Witness ___________________________

Phone _____________________________

Address ___________________________

____

Signature ________________________

Date ____________________________

LANDLORD

Name __________________________

Signature ________________________

Date __________________________ _

Address _________________________

____

Witness _________________________

Phone __________________________

Address _________________________

Signature___________Date__________

MONTH-TO-MONTH RENTAL AGREEMENT

This lease agreement is made this __________ by and (between/among) _______ ___ ___ ___ ___ ___ ___ [Landlord] and ___ ___ ___ ___ ___ ___ , [and other Tenants,] collectively [Tenant]. Each Tenant is jointly and severally liable for the payment of rent to the landlord and performance of all other terms in this Agreement.

[PREMISES]

Landlord hereby leases the premises located at ___ ___ ___ ___ ___ ___ ___ ___ ___ ___ ___ City of ___ ___ ___ ___ ___, State of ___ ___ ___ ___ ___ ___ ___ ___ ___ ___ [Premises] to Tenant.

[LEASE TERM]

The Lease will start on ___ of ___ ___ ___, 20 ___ and will continue as a month-to-month tenancy. To terminate tenancy, the Landlord or Tenant must give the other party a ___ ___ day written notice of lease non-renewal.

[LEASE PAYMENTS]

The Tenant agrees to pay Landlord for the use of the Premises in the amount of $ ___ __, payable in advance on the first day of each month, except when day falls on a legal holiday or weekend, in which case rent is due on the next business day. Rent will be paid to Landlord at Landlord's address provided herein (or to other places as directed by Landlord) by mail to ___ ___ ___ ___ ___ ___ ___ ___ ___ ___ _ __ ___ or in person, at ___ ___ ___ ___ ___ ___ ___ ___ ___ ___ ___ ___ ___ ___ __.

Landlord will accept check made payable to ______________________________________ _or cashier's check made payable to ____ __or payment by ___________________________ to______________________________

[LATE FEE]

Rent paid after the ___ ___ day of each month will be considered as late; and if rent is not paid within ___ ___ days of such due date, Tenant agrees to pay a late fee of ___ ___ ___ per day for every day that the rent is late.

[INSUFFICIENT FUNDS]

Tenant agrees to pay a charge of ___ ___ ___ for each check given by Tenant to Landlord that is returned to landlord for lack of sufficient funds.

[SECURITY DEPOSIT]

Upon execution of this Lease, Tenant shall deposit the sum of _____________to be held by the Landlord as security deposit for reasonable repair of damages to, or cleaning of the Premises upon the expiration or termination of this Lease, or other notable damages.

[USE OF PREMISES]

1. Tenant agrees that the Premises shall be used and occupied for no other purpose than as dwelling and that the Premises shall be occupied only by Tenant and the following named adults _ _ _ _ _ _ _ _ _ _ _ _ _

_ _

_ and the following named children _ _ _ _ _ _ _ _ _ _ _ _ _ _ _

_ _

_ _ _ _ _ _ _ _ _ and no other without first obtaining a written consent from the Landlord.

2. The tenant hereby agrees to be responsible for the following utilities and or services _ _ _ _ _ _ _ _ _ _ _

_ _

3. The Tenant is responsible for the following maintenance and or repairs _

_ _

4. The tenant agrees not to keep any pets on the premises without priorly obtaining a written consent from the Landlord.

[ABANDONMENT AND RIGHT TO ENTER]

In any case that the Tenant abandons the Premises during the term of this Agreement, the Landlord has the right to enter the Premises by any means necessary without facing any liability and the Landlord may terminate this Agreement.

[AMENDMENTS]

The Landlord and Tenant agree that any amendments made to this Agreement must be in writing where they must be signed by both the Landlord and the Tenant. As such any amendment made by the parties will be applied to this Agreement.

[GOVERNING LAW]

This Agreement shall be governed by and construed in accordance with the laws of _ _ _ _ _ _ _ _ _ _ _ _

_ _

TENANT

Name _

Signature _

Date _

Witness _

Phone _

Address _

_ _

Signature _

Date _

LANDLORD

Name _

Signature _

Date _

Address _

_ _

Witness _

Phone _

Address _

Signature _ _ _ _ _ _ _ _ _ _ _ _ Date _ _ _ _ _ _ _ _ _ _ _

MONTH-TO-MONTH RENTAL **AGREEMENT**

This lease agreement is made this __________ by and (between/among) _______ ___ ___ ___ ___ ___ ___ [Landlord] and ___ ___ ___ ___ ___ ___ , [and other Tenants,] collectively [Tenant]. Each Tenant is jointly and severally liable for the payment of rent to the landlord and performance of all other terms in this Agreement.

[PREMISES]

Landlord hereby leases the premises located at ___ ___ ___ ___ ___ ___ ___ ___ ___ ___ City of ___ ___ ___ ___ ___, State of ___ ___ ___ ___ ___ ___ ___ ___ [Premises] to Tenant.

[LEASE TERM]

The Lease will start on ___ of ___ ___ ___, 20 ___ and will continue as a month-to-month tenancy. To terminate tenancy, the Landlord or Tenant must give the other party a ___ ___ day written notice of lease non-renewal.

[LEASE PAYMENTS]

The Tenant agrees to pay Landlord for the use of the Premises in the amount of $ ___ __, payable in advance on the first day of each month, except when day falls on a legal holiday or weekend, in which case rent is due on the next business day. Rent will be paid to Landlord at Landlord's address provided herein (or to other places as directed by Landlord) by mail to ___ ___ ___ ___ ___ ___ ___ ___ ___ ___ _ __ ___ or in person, at ___ ___ ___ ___ ___ ___ ___ ___ ___ ___ ___ ___ ___ ___ __.

Landlord will accept check made payable to ______________________________________

_or cashier's check made payable to ______________________________________

__or payment by __________________________ to__________________________

[LATE FEE]

Rent paid after the ___ ___ day of each month will be considered as late; and if rent is not paid within ___ ___ days of such due date, Tenant agrees to pay a late fee of ___ ___ ___ per day for every day that the rent is late.

[INSUFFICIENT FUNDS]

Tenant agrees to pay a charge of ___ ___ ___ for each check given by Tenant to Landlord that is returned to landlord for lack of sufficient funds.

[SECURITY DEPOSIT]

Upon execution of this Lease, Tenant shall deposit the sum of _____________to be held by the Landlord as security deposit for reasonable repair of damages to, or cleaning of the Premises upon the expiration or termination of this Lease, or other notable damages.

[USE OF PREMISES]

1. Tenant agrees that the Premises shall be used and occupied for no other purpose than as dwelling and that the Premises shall be occupied only by Tenant and the following named adults _____________

____

_____________________________ and the following named children _______________

____

__________ and no other without first obtaining a written consent from the Landlord.

2. The tenant hereby agrees to be responsible for the following utilities and or services ___ ___ ___ _

__ ___ ___ ___ ___ ___ ___ ___ ___ ___ ___ ___ ___ _________________

3. The Tenant is responsible for the following maintenance and or repairs ___ ___ ___ ___ ___ __

_ ___ ___ ___ ___ ___ ___ ___ ___ ___ ___ ___ ___ ___ _____ ___ ___ ___ ___

4. The tenant agrees not to keep any pets on the premises without priorly obtaining a written consent from the Landlord.

[ABANDONMENT AND RIGHT TO ENTER]

In any case that the Tenant abandons the Premises during the term of this Agreement, the Landlord has the right to enter the Premises by any means necessary without facing any liability and the Landlord may terminate this Agreement.

[AMENDMENTS]

The Landlord and Tenant agree that any amendments made to this Agreement must be in writing where they must be signed by both the Landlord and the Tenant. As such any amendment made by the parties will be applied to this Agreement.

[GOVERNING LAW]

This Agreement shall be governed by and construed in accordance with the laws of ___ ___ ___ ___

___ ___ ___ ___ ___ ___ ___ ___ ___ ___ ___ ___ ___ ___ ___________________

TENANT

Name ______________________________

Signature ___________________________

Date _______________________________

Witness _____________________________

Phone ______________________________

Address _____________________________

____

Signature __________________________

Date ______________________________

LANDLORD

Name ______________________________

Signature ___________________________

Date ____________________________ _

Address _____________________________

____

Witness _____________________________

Phone _______________________________

Address _____________________________

Signature___________Date__________

MONTH-TO-MONTH RENTAL **AGREEMENT**

This lease agreement is made this __________ by and (between/among) ________ ___ ___ ___ ___ ___ ___ [Landlord] and ___ ___ ___ ___ ___ ___, [and other Tenants,] collectively [Tenant]. Each Tenant is jointly and severally liable for the payment of rent to the landlord and performance of all other terms in this Agreement.

[PREMISES]

Landlord hereby leases the premises located at ___ ___ ___ ___ ___ ___ ___ ___ ___ ___ City of ___ ___ ___ ___ ___, State of ___ ___ ___ ___ ___ ___ ___ [Premises] to Tenant.

[LEASE TERM]

The Lease will start on ___ of ___ ___ ___, 20 ___ and will continue as a month-to-month tenancy. To terminate tenancy, the Landlord or Tenant must give the other party a ___ ___ day written notice of lease non-renewal.

[LEASE PAYMENTS]

The Tenant agrees to pay Landlord for the use of the Premises in the amount of $ ___ __, payable in advance on the first day of each month, except when day falls on a legal holiday or weekend, in which case rent is due on the next business day. Rent will be paid to Landlord at Landlord's address provided herein (or to other places as directed by Landlord) by mail to ___ ___ ___ ___ ___ ___ ___ ___ ___ ___ _ __ ___ or in person, at ___ ___ ___ ___ ___ ___ ___ ___ ___ ___ ___ ___ ___ ___ __.

Landlord will accept check made payable to ______________________________________

_or cashier's check made payable to ____

__or payment by ___________________________ to__________________________

[LATE FEE]

Rent paid after the ___ ___ day of each month will be considered as late; and if rent is not paid within ___ ___ days of such due date, Tenant agrees to pay a late fee of ___ ___ ___ per day for every day that the rent is late.

[INSUFFICIENT FUNDS]

Tenant agrees to pay a charge of ___ ___ ___ for each check given by Tenant to Landlord that is returned to landlord for lack of sufficient funds.

[SECURITY DEPOSIT]

Upon execution of this Lease, Tenant shall deposit the sum of ____________to be held by the Landlord as security deposit for reasonable repair of damages to, or cleaning of the Premises upon the expiration or termination of this Lease, or other notable damages.

[USE OF PREMISES]

1. Tenant agrees that the Premises shall be used and occupied for no other purpose than as dwelling and that the Premises shall be occupied only by Tenant and the following named adults _____________

____

______________________________ and the following named children _______________

____

__________ and no other without first obtaining a written consent from the Landlord.

2. The tenant hereby agrees to be responsible for the following utilities and or services ___ ___ ___ _

__ ___ ___ ___ ___ ___ ___ ___ ___ ___ ___ ___ ___ ________________

3. The Tenant is responsible for the following maintenance and or repairs ___ ___ ___ ___ ___ __

_ ___ ___ ___ ___ ___ ___ ___ ___ ___ ___ ___ ___ _____ ___ ___ ___ ___

4. The tenant agrees not to keep any pets on the premises without priorly obtaining a written consent from the Landlord.

[ABANDONMENT AND RIGHT TO ENTER]

In any case that the Tenant abandons the Premises during the term of this Agreement, the Landlord has the right to enter the Premises by any means necessary without facing any liability and the Landlord may terminate this Agreement.

[AMENDMENTS]

The Landlord and Tenant agree that any amendments made to this Agreement must be in writing where they must be signed by both the Landlord and the Tenant. As such any amendment made by the parties will be applied to this Agreement.

[GOVERNING LAW]

This Agreement shall be governed by and construed in accordance with the laws of ___ ___ ___ ___

___ ___ ___ ___ ___ ___ ___ ___ ___ ___ ___ ___ ___ ___ __________________

TENANT

Name ______________________________

Signature __________________________

Date _______________________________

Witness ____________________________

Phone ______________________________

Address ____________________________

____

Signature __________________________

Date ______________________________

LANDLORD

Name ______________________________

Signature __________________________

Date _____________________________ _

Address ____________________________

____

Witness ____________________________

Phone ______________________________

Address ____________________________

Signature___________Date__________

MONTH-TO-MONTH RENTAL AGREEMENT

This lease agreement is made this _ _ _ _ _ _ _ _ _ _ by and (between/among) _ [Landlord] and _ _ _ _ _ _ _ _ _ _ _ _ _ _ _ _ _ _, [and other Tenants,] collectively [Tenant]. Each Tenant is jointly and severally liable for the payment of rent to the landlord and performance of all other terms in this Agreement.

[PREMISES]

Landlord hereby leases the premises located at _ City of _ _ _ _ _ _ _ _ _ _ _ _ _ _ _, State of _ [Premises] to Tenant.

[LEASE TERM]

The Lease will start on _ _ _ of _ _ _ _ _ _ _ _ _, 20 _ _ _ and will continue as a month-to-month tenancy. To terminate tenancy, the Landlord or Tenant must give the other party a _ _ _ _ _ _ day written notice of lease non-renewal.

[LEASE PAYMENTS]

The Tenant agrees to pay Landlord for the use of the Premises in the amount of $ _ _ _ _ _, payable in advance on the first day of each month, except when day falls on a legal holiday or weekend, in which case rent is due on the next business day. Rent will be paid to Landlord at Landlord's address provided herein (or to other places as directed by Landlord) by mail to _ or in person, at _.

Landlord will accept check made payable to _ or cashier's check made payable to _ or payment by _ to _

[LATE FEE]

Rent paid after the _ _ _ _ _ _ day of each month will be considered as late; and if rent is not paid within _ _ _ _ _ _ days of such due date, Tenant agrees to pay a late fee of _ _ _ _ _ _ _ _ _ per day for every day that the rent is late.

[INSUFFICIENT FUNDS]

Tenant agrees to pay a charge of _ _ _ _ _ _ _ _ _ for each check given by Tenant to Landlord that is returned to landlord for lack of sufficient funds.

[SECURITY DEPOSIT]

Upon execution of this Lease, Tenant shall deposit the sum of _ _ _ _ _ _ _ _ _ _ _ _ _ to be held by the Landlord as security deposit for reasonable repair of damages to, or cleaning of the Premises upon the expiration or termination of this Lease, or other notable damages.

[USE OF PREMISES]

1. Tenant agrees that the Premises shall be used and occupied for no other purpose than as dwelling and that the Premises shall be occupied only by Tenant and the following named adults _____________

____

______________________________ and the following named children _______________

____

__________ and no other without first obtaining a written consent from the Landlord.

2. The tenant hereby agrees to be responsible for the following utilities and or services ___ ___ ___ _

__ ___ ___ ___ ___ ___ ___ ___ ___ ___ ___ ___ ___ ___ _________________

3. The Tenant is responsible for the following maintenance and or repairs ___ ___ ___ ___ ___ __

_ ___ ___ ___ ___ ___ ___ ___ ___ ___ ___ ___ ___ ____ ___ ___ ___ ___

4. The tenant agrees not to keep any pets on the premises without priorly obtaining a written consent from the Landlord.

[ABANDONMENT AND RIGHT TO ENTER]

In any case that the Tenant abandons the Premises during the term of this Agreement, the Landlord has the right to enter the Premises by any means necessary without facing any liability and the Landlord may terminate this Agreement.

[AMENDMENTS]

The Landlord and Tenant agree that any amendments made to this Agreement must be in writing where they must be signed by both the Landlord and the Tenant. As such any amendment made by the parties will be applied to this Agreement.

[GOVERNING LAW]

This Agreement shall be governed by and construed in accordance with the laws of ___ ___ ___ ___

___ ___ ___ ___ ___ ___ ___ ___ ___ ___ ___ ___ ___ ___ ___ _________________

TENANT

Name ____________________________

Signature __________________________

Date _____________________________

Witness ___________________________

Phone ____________________________

Address ___________________________

____

Signature _________________________

Date ____________________________

LANDLORD

Name ___________________________

Signature _________________________

Date _________________________ _

Address __________________________

____

Witness __________________________

Phone ___________________________

Address __________________________

Signature___________Date__________

MONTH-TO-MONTH RENTAL **AGREEMENT**

This lease agreement is made this __________ by and (between/among) _______ ___ ___ ___ ___ ___ ___ [Landlord] and ___ ___ ___ ___ ___ ___, [and other Tenants,] collectively [Tenant]. Each Tenant is jointly and severally liable for the payment of rent to the landlord and performance of all other terms in this Agreement.

[PREMISES]

Landlord hereby leases the premises located at ___ ___ ___ ___ ___ ___ ___ ___ ___ ___ City of ___ ___ ___ ___ ___, State of ___ ___ ___ ___ ___ ___ ___ [Premises] to Tenant.

[LEASE TERM]

The Lease will start on ___ of ___ ___ ___, 20 ___ and will continue as a month-to-month tenancy. To terminate tenancy, the Landlord or Tenant must give the other party a ___ ___ day written notice of lease non-renewal.

[LEASE PAYMENTS]

The Tenant agrees to pay Landlord for the use of the Premises in the amount of $ ___ __, payable in advance on the first day of each month, except when day falls on a legal holiday or weekend, in which case rent is due on the next business day. Rent will be paid to Landlord at Landlord's address provided herein (or to other places as directed by Landlord) by mail to ___ ___ ___ ___ ___ ___ ___ ___ ___ _ __ ___ or in person, at ___ ___ ___ ___ ___ ___ ___ ___ ___ ___ ___ ___ ___ ___.
Landlord will accept check made payable to ________________________________ _or cashier's check made payable to ________________________________ __or payment by ___________________________ to___________________________

[LATE FEE]

Rent paid after the ___ ___ day of each month will be considered as late; and if rent is not paid within ___ ___ days of such due date, Tenant agrees to pay a late fee of ___ ___ ___ per day for every day that the rent is late.

[INSUFFICIENT FUNDS]

Tenant agrees to pay a charge of ___ ___ ___ for each check given by Tenant to Landlord that is returned to landlord for lack of sufficient funds.

[SECURITY DEPOSIT]

Upon execution of this Lease, Tenant shall deposit the sum of ____________to be held by the Landlord as security deposit for reasonable repair of damages to, or cleaning of the Premises upon the expiration or termination of this Lease, or other notable damages.

[USE OF PREMISES]

1. Tenant agrees that the Premises shall be used and occupied for no other purpose than as dwelling and that the Premises shall be occupied only by Tenant and the following named adults _____________

____

_______________________________ and the following named children _______________

____

__________ and no other without first obtaining a written consent from the Landlord.

2. The tenant hereby agrees to be responsible for the following utilities and or services ___ ___ ___ _

__ ___ ___ ___ ___ ___ ___ ___ ___ ___ ___ ___ ___ ___ _________________

3. The Tenant is responsible for the following maintenance and or repairs ___ ___ ___ ___ ___ __

_ ___ ___ ___ ___ ___ ___ ___ ___ ___ ___ ___ ___ ____ ___ ___ ___ ___

4. The tenant agrees not to keep any pets on the premises without priorly obtaining a written consent from the Landlord.

[ABANDONMENT AND RIGHT TO ENTER]

In any case that the Tenant abandons the Premises during the term of this Agreement, the Landlord has the right to enter the Premises by any means necessary without facing any liability and the Landlord may terminate this Agreement.

[AMENDMENTS]

The Landlord and Tenant agree that any amendments made to this Agreement must be in writing where they must be signed by both the Landlord and the Tenant. As such any amendment made by the parties will be applied to this Agreement.

[GOVERNING LAW]

This Agreement shall be governed by and construed in accordance with the laws of ___ ___ ___ ___

___ ___ ___ ___ ___ ___ ___ ___ ___ ___ ___ ___ ___ ___ ___ ___________________

TENANT

Name ____________________________

Signature __________________________

Date _____________________________

Witness ___________________________

Phone ____________________________

Address ___________________________

____

Signature _________________________

Date _____________________________

LANDLORD

Name ____________________________

Signature __________________________

Date ____________________________

Address ___________________________

____

Witness ___________________________

Phone ____________________________

Address ___________________________

Signature___________Date__________

MONTH-TO-MONTH RENTAL **AGREEMENT**

This lease agreement is made this __________ by and (between/among) _______ ___ ___ ___ ___ ___ ___ [Landlord] and ___ ___ ___ ___ ___ ___, [and other Tenants,] collectively [Tenant]. Each Tenant is jointly and severally liable for the payment of rent to the landlord and performance of all other terms in this Agreement.

[PREMISES]

Landlord hereby leases the premises located at ___ ___ ___ ___ ___ ___ ___ ___ ___ ___ City of ___ ___ ___ ___ ___, State of ___ ___ ___ ___ ___ ___ ___[Premises] to Tenant.

[LEASE TERM]

The Lease will start on ___ of ___ ___ ___, 20 ___ and will continue as a month-to-month tenancy. To terminate tenancy, the Landlord or Tenant must give the other party a ___ ___ day written notice of lease non-renewal.

[LEASE PAYMENTS]

The Tenant agrees to pay Landlord for the use of the Premises in the amount of $ ___ __, payable in advance on the first day of each month, except when day falls on a legal holiday or weekend, in which case rent is due on the next business day. Rent will be paid to Landlord at Landlord's address provided herein (or to other places as directed by Landlord) by mail to ___ ___ ___ ___ ___ ___ ___ ___ ___ ___ _ __ ___or in person, at ___ ___ ___ ___ ___ ___ ___ ___ ___ ___ ___ ___ ___ ___ __.

Landlord will accept check made payable to ________________________________ _or cashier's check made payable to __________________________________ __or payment by ___________________________ to___________________________

[LATE FEE]

Rent paid after the ___ ___ day of each month will be considered as late; and if rent is not paid within ___ ___ days of such due date, Tenant agrees to pay a late fee of ___ ___ ___ per day for every day that the rent is late.

[INSUFFICIENT FUNDS]

Tenant agrees to pay a charge of ___ ___ ___ for each check given by Tenant to Landlord that is returned to landlord for lack of sufficient funds.

[SECURITY DEPOSIT]

Upon execution of this Lease, Tenant shall deposit the sum of ____________to be held by the Landlord as security deposit for reasonable repair of damages to, or cleaning of the Premises upon the expiration or termination of this Lease, or other notable damages.

[USE OF PREMISES]

1. Tenant agrees that the Premises shall be used and occupied for no other purpose than as dwelling and that the Premises shall be occupied only by Tenant and the following named adults _ _ _ _ _ _ _ _ _ _ _ _ _

_ _

_ and the following named children _ _ _ _ _ _ _ _ _ _ _ _ _ _ _

_ _

_ _ _ _ _ _ _ _ _ _ and no other without first obtaining a written consent from the Landlord.

2. The tenant hereby agrees to be responsible for the following utilities and or services _ _ _ _ _ _ _ _ _ _ _

_ _

3. The Tenant is responsible for the following maintenance and or repairs _

_ _

4. The tenant agrees not to keep any pets on the premises without priorly obtaining a written consent from the Landlord.

[ABANDONMENT AND RIGHT TO ENTER]

In any case that the Tenant abandons the Premises during the term of this Agreement, the Landlord has the right to enter the Premises by any means necessary without facing any liability and the Landlord may terminate this Agreement.

[AMENDMENTS]

The Landlord and Tenant agree that any amendments made to this Agreement must be in writing where they must be signed by both the Landlord and the Tenant. As such any amendment made by the parties will be applied to this Agreement.

[GOVERNING LAW]

This Agreement shall be governed by and construed in accordance with the laws of _ _ _ _ _ _ _ _ _ _ _ _

_ _

TENANT

Name _

Signature _

Date _

Witness _

Phone _

Address _

_ _

Signature _

Date _

LANDLORD

Name _

Signature _

Date _

Address _

_ _

Witness _

Phone _

Address _

Signature_ _ _ _ _ _ _ _ _ _ _ _Date_ _ _ _ _ _ _ _ _ _

MONTH-TO-MONTH RENTAL AGREEMENT

This lease agreement is made this __________ by and (between/among) _______ ___ ___ ___ ___ ___ ___ [Landlord] and ___ ___ ___ ___ ___ ___, [and other Tenants,] collectively [Tenant]. Each Tenant is jointly and severally liable for the payment of rent to the landlord and performance of all other terms in this Agreement.

[PREMISES]

Landlord hereby leases the premises located at ___ ___ ___ ___ ___ ___ ___ ___ ___ ___ City of ___ ___ ___ ___ ___, State of ___ ___ ___ ___ ___ ___ ___ [Premises] to Tenant.

[LEASE TERM]

The Lease will start on ___ of ___ ___ ___, 20 ___ and will continue as a month-to-month tenancy. To terminate tenancy, the Landlord or Tenant must give the other party a ___ ___ day written notice of lease non-renewal.

[LEASE PAYMENTS]

The Tenant agrees to pay Landlord for the use of the Premises in the amount of $ ___ __, payable in advance on the first day of each month, except when day falls on a legal holiday or weekend, in which case rent is due on the next business day. Rent will be paid to Landlord at Landlord's address provided herein (or to other places as directed by Landlord) by mail to ___ ___ ___ ___ ___ ___ ___ ___ ___ ___ _ __ ___ or in person, at ___ ___ ___ ___ ___ ___ ___ ___ ___ ___ ___ ___ ___ ___ __.

Landlord will accept check made payable to ______________________________________ _or cashier's check made payable to ____ __or payment by ___________________________ to___________________________

[LATE FEE]

Rent paid after the ___ ___ day of each month will be considered as late; and if rent is not paid within ___ ___ days of such due date, Tenant agrees to pay a late fee of ___ ___ ___ per day for every day that the rent is late.

[INSUFFICIENT FUNDS]

Tenant agrees to pay a charge of ___ ___ ___ for each check given by Tenant to Landlord that is returned to landlord for lack of sufficient funds.

[SECURITY DEPOSIT]

Upon execution of this Lease, Tenant shall deposit the sum of _____________to be held by the Landlord as security deposit for reasonable repair of damages to, or cleaning of the Premises upon the expiration or termination of this Lease, or other notable damages.

[USE OF PREMISES]

1. Tenant agrees that the Premises shall be used and occupied for no other purpose than as dwelling and that the Premises shall be occupied only by Tenant and the following named adults _____________

____

______________________________ and the following named children _______________

____

__________ and no other without first obtaining a written consent from the Landlord.

2. The tenant hereby agrees to be responsible for the following utilities and or services ___ ___ ___ _

__ ___ ___ ___ ___ ___ ___ ___ ___ ___ ___ ___ ___ _________________

3. The Tenant is responsible for the following maintenance and or repairs ___ ___ ___ ___ ___ __

_ ___ ___ ___ ___ ___ ___ ___ ___ ___ ___ ___ ___ ___ _____ ___ ___ ___ ___

4. The tenant agrees not to keep any pets on the premises without priorly obtaining a written consent from the Landlord.

[ABANDONMENT AND RIGHT TO ENTER]

In any case that the Tenant abandons the Premises during the term of this Agreement, the Landlord has the right to enter the Premises by any means necessary without facing any liability and the Landlord may terminate this Agreement.

[AMENDMENTS]

The Landlord and Tenant agree that any amendments made to this Agreement must be in writing where they must be signed by both the Landlord and the Tenant. As such any amendment made by the parties will be applied to this Agreement.

[GOVERNING LAW]

This Agreement shall be governed by and construed in accordance with the laws of ___ ___ ___ ___

___ ___ ___ ___ ___ ___ ___ ___ ___ ___ ___ ___ ___ ___ ___ ___________________

TENANT

Name ______________________________

Signature __________________________

Date _______________________________

Witness ____________________________

Phone _____________________________

Address ____________________________

____

Signature __________________________

Date _____________________________

LANDLORD

Name ______________________________

Signature __________________________

Date ____________________________ _

Address ____________________________

____

Witness ____________________________

Phone ______________________________

Address ____________________________

Signature___________Date__________

MONTH-TO-MONTH RENTAL **AGREEMENT**

This lease agreement is made this __________ by and (between/among) _______ ___ ___ ___ ___ ___ ___ [Landlord] and ___ ___ ___ ___ ___ ___ , [and other Tenants,] collectively [Tenant]. Each Tenant is jointly and severally liable for the payment of rent to the landlord and performance of all other terms in this Agreement.

[PREMISES]

Landlord hereby leases the premises located at ___ ___ ___ ___ ___ ___ ___ ___ ___ ___ ___ City of ___ ___ ___ ___ ___, State of ___ ___ ___ ___ ___ ___ ___ ___ ___ [Premises] to Tenant.

[LEASE TERM]

The Lease will start on ___ of ___ ___ ___, 20 ___ and will continue as a month-to-month tenancy. To terminate tenancy, the Landlord or Tenant must give the other party a ___ ___ day written notice of lease non-renewal.

[LEASE PAYMENTS]

The Tenant agrees to pay Landlord for the use of the Premises in the amount of $ ___ __, payable in advance on the first day of each month, except when day falls on a legal holiday or weekend, in which case rent is due on the next business day. Rent will be paid to Landlord at Landlord's address provided herein (or to other places as directed by Landlord) by mail to ___ ___ ___ ___ ___ ___ ___ ___ ___ ___ _ __ ___ or in person, at ___ ___ ___ ___ ___ ___ ___ ___ ___ ___ ___ ___ ___ ___ __.

Landlord will accept check made payable to ____

_or cashier's check made payable to ____

__or payment by ____________________________ to_________________________

[LATE FEE]

Rent paid after the ___ ___ day of each month will be considered as late; and if rent is not paid within ___ ___ days of such due date, Tenant agrees to pay a late fee of ___ ___ ___ per day for every day that the rent is late.

[INSUFFICIENT FUNDS]

Tenant agrees to pay a charge of ___ ___ ___ for each check given by Tenant to Landlord that is returned to landlord for lack of sufficient funds.

[SECURITY DEPOSIT]

Upon execution of this Lease, Tenant shall deposit the sum of _____________to be held by the Landlord as security deposit for reasonable repair of damages to, or cleaning of the Premises upon the expiration or termination of this Lease, or other notable damages.

[USE OF PREMISES]

1. Tenant agrees that the Premises shall be used and occupied for no other purpose than as dwelling and that the Premises shall be occupied only by Tenant and the following named adults _____________

____

_____________________________ and the following named children _______________

____

__________ and no other without first obtaining a written consent from the Landlord.

2. The tenant hereby agrees to be responsible for the following utilities and or services ___ ___ ___ _

__ ___ ___ ___ ___ ___ ___ ___ ___ ___ ___ ___ ___ ___ _________________

3. The Tenant is responsible for the following maintenance and or repairs ___ ___ ___ ___ ___ __

_ ___ ___ ___ ___ ___ ___ ___ ___ ___ ___ ___ ___ _____ ___ ___ ___ ___

4. The tenant agrees not to keep any pets on the premises without priorly obtaining a written consent from the Landlord.

[ABANDONMENT AND RIGHT TO ENTER]

In any case that the Tenant abandons the Premises during the term of this Agreement, the Landlord has the right to enter the Premises by any means necessary without facing any liability and the Landlord may terminate this Agreement.

[AMENDMENTS]

The Landlord and Tenant agree that any amendments made to this Agreement must be in writing where they must be signed by both the Landlord and the Tenant. As such any amendment made by the parties will be applied to this Agreement.

[GOVERNING LAW]

This Agreement shall be governed by and construed in accordance with the laws of ___ ___ ___ ___

___ ___ ___ ___ ___ ___ ___ ___ ___ ___ ___ ___ ___ ___ ___ ____________________

TENANT

Name ______________________________

Signature __________________________

Date ______________________________

Witness ____________________________

Phone _____________________________

Address ____________________________

____

Signature __________________________

Date ______________________________

LANDLORD

Name ______________________________

Signature __________________________

Date _____________________________ _

Address ____________________________

____

Witness ____________________________

Phone ______________________________

Address ____________________________

Signature___________Date__________

MONTH-TO-MONTH RENTAL **AGREEMENT**

This lease agreement is made this __________ by and (between/among) _______ ___ ___ ___ ___ ___ ___ [Landlord] and ___ ___ ___ ___ ___ ___, [and other Tenants,] collectively [Tenant]. Each Tenant is jointly and severally liable for the payment of rent to the landlord and performance of all other terms in this Agreement.

[PREMISES]

Landlord hereby leases the premises located at ___ ___ ___ ___ ___ ___ ___ ___ ___ ___ City of ___ ___ ___ ___ ___, State of ___ ___ ___ ___ ___ ___ ___ ___ [Premises] to Tenant.

[LEASE TERM]

The Lease will start on ___ of ___ ___ ___, 20 ___ and will continue as a month-to-month tenancy. To terminate tenancy, the Landlord or Tenant must give the other party a ___ ___ day written notice of lease non-renewal.

[LEASE PAYMENTS]

The Tenant agrees to pay Landlord for the use of the Premises in the amount of $ ___ __, payable in advance on the first day of each month, except when day falls on a legal holiday or weekend, in which case rent is due on the next business day. Rent will be paid to Landlord at Landlord's address provided herein (or to other places as directed by Landlord) by mail to ___ ___ ___ ___ ___ ___ ___ ___ ___ ___ _ __ ___ or in person, at ___ ___ ___ ___ ___ ___ ___ ___ ___ ___ ___ ___ ___ ___ __.

Landlord will accept check made payable to ___________________________________

_or cashier's check made payable to ___________________________________

__or payment by ___________________________ to___________________________

[LATE FEE]

Rent paid after the ___ ___ day of each month will be considered as late; and if rent is not paid within ___ ___ days of such due date, Tenant agrees to pay a late fee of ___ ___ ___ per day for every day that the rent is late.

[INSUFFICIENT FUNDS]

Tenant agrees to pay a charge of ___ ___ ___ for each check given by Tenant to Landlord that is returned to landlord for lack of sufficient funds.

[SECURITY DEPOSIT]

Upon execution of this Lease, Tenant shall deposit the sum of _____________to be held by the Landlord as security deposit for reasonable repair of damages to, or cleaning of the Premises upon the expiration or termination of this Lease, or other notable damages.

[USE OF PREMISES]

1. Tenant agrees that the Premises shall be used and occupied for no other purpose than as dwelling and that the Premises shall be occupied only by Tenant and the following named adults _____________

____

_____________________________ and the following named children _______________

____

__________ and no other without first obtaining a written consent from the Landlord.

2. The tenant hereby agrees to be responsible for the following utilities and or services ___ ___ ___ _

__ ___ ___ ___ ___ ___ ___ ___ ___ ___ ___ ___ ___ _______________

3. The Tenant is responsible for the following maintenance and or repairs ___ ___ ___ ___ ___ __

_ ___ ___ ___ ___ ___ ___ ___ ___ ___ ___ ___ ___ _____ ___ ___ ___ ___

4. The tenant agrees not to keep any pets on the premises without priorly obtaining a written consent from the Landlord.

[ABANDONMENT AND RIGHT TO ENTER]

In any case that the Tenant abandons the Premises during the term of this Agreement, the Landlord has the right to enter the Premises by any means necessary without facing any liability and the Landlord may terminate this Agreement.

[AMENDMENTS]

The Landlord and Tenant agree that any amendments made to this Agreement must be in writing where they must be signed by both the Landlord and the Tenant. As such any amendment made by the parties will be applied to this Agreement.

[GOVERNING LAW]

This Agreement shall be governed by and construed in accordance with the laws of ___ ___ ___ ___

___ ___ ___ ___ ___ ___ ___ ___ ___ ___ ___ ___ ___ ___ ________________

TENANT

Name ____________________________

Signature _________________________

Date _____________________________

Witness ___________________________

Phone ____________________________

Address ___________________________

____

Signature ________________________

Date ____________________________

LANDLORD

Name ____________________________

Signature _________________________

Date ___________________________ _

Address ___________________________

____

Witness ___________________________

Phone ____________________________

Address ___________________________

Signature___________Date__________

MONTH-TO-MONTH RENTAL AGREEMENT

This lease agreement is made this _ _ _ _ _ _ _ _ _ _ by and (between/among) _ [Landlord] and _, [and other Tenants,] collectively [Tenant]. Each Tenant is jointly and severally liable for the payment of rent to the landlord and performance of all other terms in this Agreement.

[PREMISES]

Landlord hereby leases the premises located at _ City of _ _ _ _ _ _ _ _ _ _ _ _ _ _ _, State of _ [Premises] to Tenant.

[LEASE TERM]

The Lease will start on _ _ _ of _ _ _ _ _ _ _ _ _, 20 _ _ _ and will continue as a month-to-month tenancy. To terminate tenancy, the Landlord or Tenant must give the other party a _ _ _ _ _ _ day written notice of lease non-renewal.

[LEASE PAYMENTS]

The Tenant agrees to pay Landlord for the use of the Premises in the amount of $ _ _ _ _ _, payable in advance on the first day of each month, except when day falls on a legal holiday or weekend, in which case rent is due on the next business day. Rent will be paid to Landlord at Landlord's address provided herein (or to other places as directed by Landlord) by mail to _ or in person, at _.
Landlord will accept check made payable to _ or cashier's check made payable to _ or payment by _ to _

[LATE FEE]

Rent paid after the _ _ _ _ _ _ day of each month will be considered as late; and if rent is not paid within _ _ _ _ _ _ days of such due date, Tenant agrees to pay a late fee of _ _ _ _ _ _ _ _ _ per day for every day that the rent is late.

[INSUFFICIENT FUNDS]

Tenant agrees to pay a charge of _ _ _ _ _ _ _ _ _ for each check given by Tenant to Landlord that is returned to landlord for lack of sufficient funds.

[SECURITY DEPOSIT]

Upon execution of this Lease, Tenant shall deposit the sum of _ _ _ _ _ _ _ _ _ _ _ _ _ to be held by the Landlord as security deposit for reasonable repair of damages to, or cleaning of the Premises upon the expiration or termination of this Lease, or other notable damages.

[USE OF PREMISES]

1. Tenant agrees that the Premises shall be used and occupied for no other purpose than as dwelling and that the Premises shall be occupied only by Tenant and the following named adults _____________

____

______________________________ and the following named children ______________

____

__________ and no other without first obtaining a written consent from the Landlord.

2. The tenant hereby agrees to be responsible for the following utilities and or services ___ ___ ___ _

__ ___ ___ ___ ___ ___ ___ ___ ___ ___ ___ ___ ___ __________________

3. The Tenant is responsible for the following maintenance and or repairs ___ ___ ___ ___ ___ __

_ ___ ___ ___ ___ ___ ___ ___ ___ ___ ___ ___ ___ ____ ___ ___ ___ ___

4. The tenant agrees not to keep any pets on the premises without priorly obtaining a written consent from the Landlord.

[ABANDONMENT AND RIGHT TO ENTER]

In any case that the Tenant abandons the Premises during the term of this Agreement, the Landlord has the right to enter the Premises by any means necessary without facing any liability and the Landlord may terminate this Agreement.

[AMENDMENTS]

The Landlord and Tenant agree that any amendments made to this Agreement must be in writing where they must be signed by both the Landlord and the Tenant. As such any amendment made by the parties will be applied to this Agreement.

[GOVERNING LAW]

This Agreement shall be governed by and construed in accordance with the laws of ___ ___ ___ ___

___ ___ ___ ___ ___ ___ ___ ___ ___ ___ ___ ___ ___ ____________________

TENANT

Name ______________________________

Signature ___________________________

Date _______________________________

Witness ____________________________

Phone ______________________________

Address ____________________________

____

Signature ___________________________

Date _______________________________

LANDLORD

Name ______________________________

Signature ___________________________

Date _____________________________ _

Address ____________________________

____

Witness ____________________________

Phone ______________________________

Address ____________________________

Signature____________Date__________

MONTH-TO-MONTH RENTAL AGREEMENT

This lease agreement is made this __________ by and (between/among) _______ ___ ___ ___

___ ___ ___ [Landlord] and ___ ___ ___ ___ ___ ___, [and other Tenants,] collectively [Tenant]. Each Tenant is jointly and severally liable for the payment of rent to the landlord and performance of all other terms in this Agreement.

[PREMISES]

Landlord hereby leases the premises located at ___ ___ ___ ___ ___ ___ ___ ___ ___ ___

City of ___ ___ ___ ___ ___, State of ___ ___ ___ ___ ___ ___ ___ [Premises] to Tenant.

[LEASE TERM]

The Lease will start on ___ of ___ ___ ___, 20 ___ and will continue as a month-to-month tenancy. To terminate tenancy, the Landlord or Tenant must give the other party a ___ ___ day written notice of lease non-renewal.

[LEASE PAYMENTS]

The Tenant agrees to pay Landlord for the use of the Premises in the amount of $ ___ __, payable in advance on the first day of each month, except when day falls on a legal holiday or weekend, in which case rent is due on the next business day. Rent will be paid to Landlord at Landlord's address provided herein (or to other places as directed by Landlord) by mail to ___ ___ ___ ___ ___ ___ ___ ___ ___ ___ _

__ ___ or in person, at ___ ___ ___ ___ ___ ___ ___ ___ ___ ___ ___ ___ ___ ___ ___.

Landlord will accept check made payable to ______________________________

_or cashier's check made payable to ______________________________

__or payment by ___________________________ to___________________________

[LATE FEE]

Rent paid after the ___ ___ day of each month will be considered as late; and if rent is not paid within ___ ___ days of such due date, Tenant agrees to pay a late fee of ___ ___ ___ per day for every day that the rent is late.

[INSUFFICIENT FUNDS]

Tenant agrees to pay a charge of ___ ___ ___ for each check given by Tenant to Landlord that is returned to landlord for lack of sufficient funds.

[SECURITY DEPOSIT]

Upon execution of this Lease, Tenant shall deposit the sum of _____________to be held by the Landlord as security deposit for reasonable repair of damages to, or cleaning of the Premises upon the expiration or termination of this Lease, or other notable damages.

[USE OF PREMISES]

1. Tenant agrees that the Premises shall be used and occupied for no other purpose than as dwelling and that the Premises shall be occupied only by Tenant and the following named adults _____________

____

______________________________ and the following named children ________________

____

__________ and no other without first obtaining a written consent from the Landlord.

2. The tenant hereby agrees to be responsible for the following utilities and or services ___ ___ ___ _

____

3. The Tenant is responsible for the following maintenance and or repairs ___ ___ ___ ___ ___ __

____

4. The tenant agrees not to keep any pets on the premises without priorly obtaining a written consent from the Landlord.

[ABANDONMENT AND RIGHT TO ENTER]

In any case that the Tenant abandons the Premises during the term of this Agreement, the Landlord has the right to enter the Premises by any means necessary without facing any liability and the Landlord may terminate this Agreement.

[AMENDMENTS]

The Landlord and Tenant agree that any amendments made to this Agreement must be in writing where they must be signed by both the Landlord and the Tenant. As such any amendment made by the parties will be applied to this Agreement.

[GOVERNING LAW]

This Agreement shall be governed by and construed in accordance with the laws of ___ ___ ___ ___

____

TENANT

Name ______________________________

Signature ___________________________

Date _______________________________

Witness _____________________________

Phone ______________________________

Address _____________________________

____

Signature ___________________________

Date _______________________________

LANDLORD

Name ______________________________

Signature ___________________________

Date _______________________________

Address _____________________________

____

Witness _____________________________

Phone ______________________________

Address _____________________________

Signature____________Date__________

MONTH-TO-MONTH RENTAL **AGREEMENT**

This lease agreement is made this __________ by and (between/among) ________ ___ ___ ___ ___ ___ ___ [Landlord] and ___ ___ ___ ___ ___ ___ , [and other Tenants,] collectively [Tenant]. Each Tenant is jointly and severally liable for the payment of rent to the landlord and performance of all other terms in this Agreement.

[PREMISES]

Landlord hereby leases the premises located at ___ ___ ___ ___ ___ ___ ___ ___ ___ ___ City of ___ ___ ___ ___ ___ , State of ___ ___ ___ ___ ___ ___ ___ [Premises] to Tenant.

[LEASE TERM]

The Lease will start on ___ of ___ ___ ___ , 20 ___ and will continue as a month-to-month tenancy. To terminate tenancy, the Landlord or Tenant must give the other party a ___ ___ day written notice of lease non-renewal.

[LEASE PAYMENTS]

The Tenant agrees to pay Landlord for the use of the Premises in the amount of $ ___ __, payable in advance on the first day of each month, except when day falls on a legal holiday or weekend, in which case rent is due on the next business day. Rent will be paid to Landlord at Landlord's address provided herein (or to other places as directed by Landlord) by mail to ___ ___ ___ ___ ___ ___ ___ ___ ___ ___ _ __ ___ or in person, at ___ ___ ___ ___ ___ ___ ___ ___ ___ ___ ___ ___ __.

Landlord will accept check made payable to ___________________________

_or cashier's check made payable to ___________________________

__or payment by ___________________________ to___________________________

[LATE FEE]

Rent paid after the ___ ___ day of each month will be considered as late; and if rent is not paid within ___ ___ days of such due date, Tenant agrees to pay a late fee of ___ ___ ___ per day for every day that the rent is late.

[INSUFFICIENT FUNDS]

Tenant agrees to pay a charge of ___ ___ ___ for each check given by Tenant to Landlord that is returned to landlord for lack of sufficient funds.

[SECURITY DEPOSIT]

Upon execution of this Lease, Tenant shall deposit the sum of _____________to be held by the Landlord as security deposit for reasonable repair of damages to, or cleaning of the Premises upon the expiration or termination of this Lease, or other notable damages.

[USE OF PREMISES]

1. Tenant agrees that the Premises shall be used and occupied for no other purpose than as dwelling and that the Premises shall be occupied only by Tenant and the following named adults _____________

____

_____________________________ and the following named children _______________

____

__________ and no other without first obtaining a written consent from the Landlord.

2. The tenant hereby agrees to be responsible for the following utilities and or services ___ ___ ____ _

__ ___ ___ ___ ___ ___ ___ ___ ___ ___ ___ ___ ___ ___ ___ ___ _____________

3. The Tenant is responsible for the following maintenance and or repairs ___ ___ ___ ___ ___ __

_ ___ ___ ___ ___ ___ ___ ___ ___ ___ ___ ___ ___ _____ ___ ___ ___ ___

4. The tenant agrees not to keep any pets on the premises without priorly obtaining a written consent from the Landlord.

[ABANDONMENT AND RIGHT TO ENTER]

In any case that the Tenant abandons the Premises during the term of this Agreement, the Landlord has the right to enter the Premises by any means necessary without facing any liability and the Landlord may terminate this Agreement.

[AMENDMENTS]

The Landlord and Tenant agree that any amendments made to this Agreement must be in writing where they must be signed by both the Landlord and the Tenant. As such any amendment made by the parties will be applied to this Agreement.

[GOVERNING LAW]

This Agreement shall be governed by and construed in accordance with the laws of ___ ___ ___ ___

___ ___ ___ ___ ___ ___ ___ ___ ___ ___ ___ ___ ___ _________________

TENANT

Name ____________________________

Signature __________________________

Date _____________________________

Witness ___________________________

Phone ____________________________

Address ___________________________

____

Signature ________________________

Date ___________________________

LANDLORD

Name __________________________

Signature ________________________

Date _________________________ _

Address ________________________

____

Witness ________________________

Phone __________________________

Address ________________________

Signature____________Date__________

MONTH-TO-MONTH RENTAL **AGREEMENT**

This lease agreement is made this ___________ by and (between/among) _______ ___ ___ ___ ___ ___ ___ [Landlord] and ___ ___ ___ ___ ___ ___ ___, [and other Tenants,] collectively [Tenant]. Each Tenant is jointly and severally liable for the payment of rent to the landlord and performance of all other terms in this Agreement.

[PREMISES]

Landlord hereby leases the premises located at ___ ___ ___ ___ ___ ___ ___ ___ ___ ___

City of ___ ___ ___ ___ ___, State of ___ ___ ___ ___ ___ ___ ___ ___ [Premises] to Tenant.

[LEASE TERM]

The Lease will start on ___ of ___ ___ ___, 20 ___ and will continue as a month-to-month tenancy. To terminate tenancy, the Landlord or Tenant must give the other party a ___ ___ day written notice of lease non-renewal.

[LEASE PAYMENTS]

The Tenant agrees to pay Landlord for the use of the Premises in the amount of $ ___ __, payable in advance on the first day of each month, except when day falls on a legal holiday or weekend, in which case rent is due on the next business day. Rent will be paid to Landlord at Landlord's address provided herein (or to other places as directed by Landlord) by mail to ___ ___ ___ ___ ___ ___ ___ ___ ___ ___ _ __ ___ or in person, at ___ ___ ___ ___ ___ ___ ___ ___ ___ ___ ___ ___ ___ ___.

Landlord will accept check made payable to ______________________________

_or cashier's check made payable to ______________________________

__or payment by ____________________________ to____________________________

[LATE FEE]

Rent paid after the ___ ___ day of each month will be considered as late; and if rent is not paid within ___ ___ days of such due date, Tenant agrees to pay a late fee of ___ ___ ___ per day for every day that the rent is late.

[INSUFFICIENT FUNDS]

Tenant agrees to pay a charge of ___ ___ ___ for each check given by Tenant to Landlord that is returned to landlord for lack of sufficient funds.

[SECURITY DEPOSIT]

Upon execution of this Lease, Tenant shall deposit the sum of _____________to be held by the Landlord as security deposit for reasonable repair of damages to, or cleaning of the Premises upon the expiration or termination of this Lease, or other notable damages.

[USE OF PREMISES]

1. Tenant agrees that the Premises shall be used and occupied for no other purpose than as dwelling and that the Premises shall be occupied only by Tenant and the following named adults _____________

____

____________________________ and the following named children _______________

____

__________ and no other without first obtaining a written consent from the Landlord.

2. The tenant hereby agrees to be responsible for the following utilities and or services ___ ___ ___ _

__ ___ ___ ___ ___ ___ ___ ___ ___ ___ ___ ___ ___ _________________

3. The Tenant is responsible for the following maintenance and or repairs ___ ___ ___ ___ ___ __

_ ___ ___ ___ ___ ___ ___ ___ ___ ___ ___ ___ ___ _____ ___ ___ ___ ___

4. The tenant agrees not to keep any pets on the premises without priorly obtaining a written consent from the Landlord.

[ABANDONMENT AND RIGHT TO ENTER]

In any case that the Tenant abandons the Premises during the term of this Agreement, the Landlord has the right to enter the Premises by any means necessary without facing any liability and the Landlord may terminate this Agreement.

[AMENDMENTS]

The Landlord and Tenant agree that any amendments made to this Agreement must be in writing where they must be signed by both the Landlord and the Tenant. As such any amendment made by the parties will be applied to this Agreement.

[GOVERNING LAW]

This Agreement shall be governed by and construed in accordance with the laws of ___ ___ ___ ___

___ ___ ___ ___ ___ ___ ___ ___ ___ ___ ___ ___ ___ ___ ___ ___________________

TENANT

Name ______________________________

Signature ___________________________

Date _______________________________

Witness ____________________________

Phone ______________________________

Address ____________________________

____

Signature __________________________

Date ______________________________

LANDLORD

Name ______________________________

Signature ___________________________

Date ____________________________ _

Address ____________________________

____

Witness ____________________________

Phone ______________________________

Address ____________________________

Signature___________Date__________

MONTH-TO-MONTH RENTAL **AGREEMENT**

This lease agreement is made this __________ by and (between/among) _______ ___ ___ ___ ___ ___ ___ [Landlord] and ___ ___ ___ ___ ___ ___, [and other Tenants,] collectively [Tenant]. Each Tenant is jointly and severally liable for the payment of rent to the landlord and performance of all other terms in this Agreement.

[PREMISES]

Landlord hereby leases the premises located at ___ ___ ___ ___ ___ ___ ___ ___ ___ ___ City of ___ ___ ___ ___ ___, State of ___ ___ ___ ___ ___ ___ ___ [Premises] to Tenant.

[LEASE TERM]

The Lease will start on ___ of ___ ___ ___, 20 ___ and will continue as a month-to-month tenancy. To terminate tenancy, the Landlord or Tenant must give the other party a ___ ___ day written notice of lease non-renewal.

[LEASE PAYMENTS]

The Tenant agrees to pay Landlord for the use of the Premises in the amount of $ ___ __, payable in advance on the first day of each month, except when day falls on a legal holiday or weekend, in which case rent is due on the next business day. Rent will be paid to Landlord at Landlord's address provided herein (or to other places as directed by Landlord) by mail to ___ ___ ___ ___ ___ ___ ___ ___ ___ ___ _ __ ___ or in person, at ___ ___ ___ ___ ___ ___ ___ ___ ___ ___ ___ ___ ___ ___.
Landlord will accept check made payable to ____
_or cashier's check made payable to ____
__or payment by ___________________________ to___________________________

[LATE FEE]

Rent paid after the ___ ___ day of each month will be considered as late; and if rent is not paid within ___ ___ days of such due date, Tenant agrees to pay a late fee of ___ ___ ___ per day for every day that the rent is late.

[INSUFFICIENT FUNDS]

Tenant agrees to pay a charge of ___ ___ ___ for each check given by Tenant to Landlord that is returned to landlord for lack of sufficient funds.

[SECURITY DEPOSIT]

Upon execution of this Lease, Tenant shall deposit the sum of _____________to be held by the Landlord as security deposit for reasonable repair of damages to, or cleaning of the Premises upon the expiration or termination of this Lease, or other notable damages.

[USE OF PREMISES]

1. Tenant agrees that the Premises shall be used and occupied for no other purpose than as dwelling and that the Premises shall be occupied only by Tenant and the following named adults _____________

____

_____________________________ and the following named children ______________

____

__________ and no other without first obtaining a written consent from the Landlord.

2. The tenant hereby agrees to be responsible for the following utilities and or services ___ ___ ___ _

__ ___ ___ ___ ___ ___ ___ ___ ___ ___ ___ ___ ___ ________________

3. The Tenant is responsible for the following maintenance and or repairs ___ ___ ___ ___ ___ __

_ ___ ___ ___ ___ ___ ___ ___ ___ ___ ___ ___ ___ ____ ___ ___ ___ ___

4. The tenant agrees not to keep any pets on the premises without priorly obtaining a written consent from the Landlord.

[ABANDONMENT AND RIGHT TO ENTER]

In any case that the Tenant abandons the Premises during the term of this Agreement, the Landlord has the right to enter the Premises by any means necessary without facing any liability and the Landlord may terminate this Agreement.

[AMENDMENTS]

The Landlord and Tenant agree that any amendments made to this Agreement must be in writing where they must be signed by both the Landlord and the Tenant. As such any amendment made by the parties will be applied to this Agreement.

[GOVERNING LAW]

This Agreement shall be governed by and construed in accordance with the laws of ___ ___ ___ ___

___ ___ ___ ___ ___ ___ ___ ___ ___ ___ ___ ___ ___ ___ ___________________

TENANT

Name ______________________________

Signature ___________________________

Date _______________________________

Witness _____________________________

Phone ______________________________

Address _____________________________

____

Signature __________________________

Date ______________________________

LANDLORD

Name ____________________________

Signature __________________________

Date _________________________ _

Address __________________________

____

Witness __________________________

Phone _____________________________

Address ___________________________

Signature___________Date__________

MONTH-TO-MONTH RENTAL **AGREEMENT**

This lease agreement is made this __________ by and (between/among) _______ ___ ___ ___ ___ ___ ___ [Landlord] and ___ ___ ___ ___ ___ ___ , [and other Tenants,] collectively [Tenant]. Each Tenant is jointly and severally liable for the payment of rent to the landlord and performance of all other terms in this Agreement.

[PREMISES]

Landlord hereby leases the premises located at ___ ___ ___ ___ ___ ___ ___ ___ ___ ___ City of ___ ___ ___ ___ ___, State of ___ ___ ___ ___ ___ ___ ___ [Premises] to Tenant.

[LEASE TERM]

The Lease will start on ___ of ___ ___ ___, 20 ___ and will continue as a month-to-month tenancy. To terminate tenancy, the Landlord or Tenant must give the other party a ___ ___ day written notice of lease non-renewal.

[LEASE PAYMENTS]

The Tenant agrees to pay Landlord for the use of the Premises in the amount of $ ___ __, payable in advance on the first day of each month, except when day falls on a legal holiday or weekend, in which case rent is due on the next business day. Rent will be paid to Landlord at Landlord's address provided herein (or to other places as directed by Landlord) by mail to ___ ___ ___ ___ ___ ___ ___ ___ ___ ___ _ __ ___ or in person, at ___ ___ ___ ___ ___ ___ ___ ___ ___ ___ ___ ___ ___ ___ __.
Landlord will accept check made payable to ______________________________________ _or cashier's check made payable to ______________________________________ __or payment by ___________________________ to___________________________

[LATE FEE]

Rent paid after the ___ ___ day of each month will be considered as late; and if rent is not paid within ___ ___ days of such due date, Tenant agrees to pay a late fee of ___ ___ ___ per day for every day that the rent is late.

[INSUFFICIENT FUNDS]

Tenant agrees to pay a charge of ___ ___ ___ for each check given by Tenant to Landlord that is returned to landlord for lack of sufficient funds.

[SECURITY DEPOSIT]

Upon execution of this Lease, Tenant shall deposit the sum of _____________to be held by the Landlord as security deposit for reasonable repair of damages to, or cleaning of the Premises upon the expiration or termination of this Lease, or other notable damages.

[USE OF PREMISES]

1. Tenant agrees that the Premises shall be used and occupied for no other purpose than as dwelling and that the Premises shall be occupied only by Tenant and the following named adults _____________

____

_____________________________ and the following named children _______________

____

__________ and no other without first obtaining a written consent from the Landlord.

2. The tenant hereby agrees to be responsible for the following utilities and or services ___ ___ ___ _

__ ___ ___ ___ ___ ___ ___ ___ ___ ___ ___ ___ ___ _______________

3. The Tenant is responsible for the following maintenance and or repairs ___ ___ ___ ___ ___ __

_ ___ ___ ___ ___ ___ ___ ___ ___ ___ ___ ___ ___ _____ ___ ___ ___ ___

4. The tenant agrees not to keep any pets on the premises without priorly obtaining a written consent from the Landlord.

[ABANDONMENT AND RIGHT TO ENTER]

In any case that the Tenant abandons the Premises during the term of this Agreement, the Landlord has the right to enter the Premises by any means necessary without facing any liability and the Landlord may terminate this Agreement.

[AMENDMENTS]

The Landlord and Tenant agree that any amendments made to this Agreement must be in writing where they must be signed by both the Landlord and the Tenant. As such any amendment made by the parties will be applied to this Agreement.

[GOVERNING LAW]

This Agreement shall be governed by and construed in accordance with the laws of ___ ___ ___ ___

___ ___ ___ ___ ___ ___ ___ ___ ___ ___ ___ ___ ___ ___ _______________

TENANT

Name ____________________________

Signature ________________________

Date _____________________________

Witness __________________________

Phone ____________________________

Address __________________________

____

Signature ________________________

Date _____________________________

LANDLORD

Name __________________________

Signature ______________________

Date __________________________

Address ________________________

____

Witness ________________________

Phone __________________________

Address ________________________

Signature___________Date__________

MONTH-TO-MONTH RENTAL **AGREEMENT**

This lease agreement is made this __________ by and (between/among) _______ ___ ___ ___ ___ ___ ___ [Landlord] and ___ ___ ___ ___ ___ ___, [and other Tenants,] collectively [Tenant]. Each Tenant is jointly and severally liable for the payment of rent to the landlord and performance of all other terms in this Agreement.

[PREMISES]

Landlord hereby leases the premises located at ___ ___ ___ ___ ___ ___ ___ ___ ___ ___ City of ___ ___ ___ ___ ___, State of ___ ___ ___ ___ ___ ___ ___ ___ [Premises] to Tenant.

[LEASE TERM]

The Lease will start on ___ of ___ ___ ___, 20 ___ and will continue as a month-to-month tenancy. To terminate tenancy, the Landlord or Tenant must give the other party a ___ ___ day written notice of lease non-renewal.

[LEASE PAYMENTS]

The Tenant agrees to pay Landlord for the use of the Premises in the amount of $ ___ __, payable in advance on the first day of each month, except when day falls on a legal holiday or weekend, in which case rent is due on the next business day. Rent will be paid to Landlord at Landlord's address provided herein (or to other places as directed by Landlord) by mail to ___ ___ ___ ___ ___ ___ ___ ___ ___ ___ _ __ ___or in person, at ___ ___ ___ ___ ___ ___ ___ ___ ___ ___ ___ ___ ___ ___ __.
Landlord will accept check made payable to ______________________________
_or cashier's check made payable to ______________________________
__or payment by ___________________________to_____________________________

[LATE FEE]

Rent paid after the ___ ___ day of each month will be considered as late; and if rent is not paid within ___ ___ days of such due date, Tenant agrees to pay a late fee of ___ ___ ___ per day for every day that the rent is late.

[INSUFFICIENT FUNDS]

Tenant agrees to pay a charge of ___ ___ ___ for each check given by Tenant to Landlord that is returned to landlord for lack of sufficient funds.

[SECURITY DEPOSIT]

Upon execution of this Lease, Tenant shall deposit the sum of _____________to be held by the Landlord as security deposit for reasonable repair of damages to, or cleaning of the Premises upon the expiration or termination of this Lease, or other notable damages.

[USE OF PREMISES]

1. Tenant agrees that the Premises shall be used and occupied for no other purpose than as dwelling and that the Premises shall be occupied only by Tenant and the following named adults _____________

____

___________________________ and the following named children _______________

____

__________ and no other without first obtaining a written consent from the Landlord.

2. The tenant hereby agrees to be responsible for the following utilities and or services ___ ___ ___ _

__ ___ ___ ___ ___ ___ ___ ___ ___ ___ ___ ___ ___ ___ _________________

3. The Tenant is responsible for the following maintenance and or repairs ___ ___ ___ ___ ___ __

_ ___ ___ ___ ___ ___ ___ ___ ___ ___ ___ ___ ___ _____ ___ ___ ___ ___

4. The tenant agrees not to keep any pets on the premises without priorly obtaining a written consent from the Landlord.

[ABANDONMENT AND RIGHT TO ENTER]

In any case that the Tenant abandons the Premises during the term of this Agreement, the Landlord has the right to enter the Premises by any means necessary without facing any liability and the Landlord may terminate this Agreement.

[AMENDMENTS]

The Landlord and Tenant agree that any amendments made to this Agreement must be in writing where they must be signed by both the Landlord and the Tenant. As such any amendment made by the parties will be applied to this Agreement.

[GOVERNING LAW]

This Agreement shall be governed by and construed in accordance with the laws of ___ ___ ___ ___

___ ___ ___ ___ ___ ___ ___ ___ ___ ___ ___ ___ ___ ___ ___ ___________________

TENANT

Name ______________________________

Signature ___________________________

Date _______________________________

Witness _____________________________

Phone ______________________________

Address _____________________________

____

Signature __________________________

Date ______________________________

LANDLORD

Name ______________________________

Signature ___________________________

Date ____________________________ _

Address _____________________________

____

Witness _____________________________

Phone _______________________________

Address _____________________________

Signature___________Date__________

MONTH-TO-MONTH RENTAL AGREEMENT

This lease agreement is made this __________ by and (between/among) _______ ___ ___ ___ ___ ___ ___ [Landlord] and ___ ___ ___ ___ ___ ___, [and other Tenants,] collectively [Tenant]. Each Tenant is jointly and severally liable for the payment of rent to the landlord and performance of all other terms in this Agreement.

[PREMISES]

Landlord hereby leases the premises located at ___ ___ ___ ___ ___ ___ ___ ___ ___ ___ City of ___ ___ ___ ___ ___, State of ___ ___ ___ ___ ___ ___ ___ [Premises] to Tenant.

[LEASE TERM]

The Lease will start on ___ of ___ ___ ___, 20 ___ and will continue as a month-to-month tenancy. To terminate tenancy, the Landlord or Tenant must give the other party a ___ ___ day written notice of lease non-renewal.

[LEASE PAYMENTS]

The Tenant agrees to pay Landlord for the use of the Premises in the amount of $ ___ __, payable in advance on the first day of each month, except when day falls on a legal holiday or weekend, in which case rent is due on the next business day. Rent will be paid to Landlord at Landlord's address provided herein (or to other places as directed by Landlord) by mail to ___ ___ ___ ___ ___ ___ ___ ___ ___ ___ _ __ ___ or in person, at ___ ___ ___ ___ ___ ___ ___ ___ ___ ___ ___ ___ ___ ___ __ .

Landlord will accept check made payable to ____ _or cashier's check made payable to ____ __or payment by ___________________________ to___________________________

[LATE FEE]

Rent paid after the ___ ___ day of each month will be considered as late; and if rent is not paid within ___ ___ days of such due date, Tenant agrees to pay a late fee of ___ ___ ___ per day for every day that the rent is late.

[INSUFFICIENT FUNDS]

Tenant agrees to pay a charge of ___ ___ ___ for each check given by Tenant to Landlord that is returned to landlord for lack of sufficient funds.

[SECURITY DEPOSIT]

Upon execution of this Lease, Tenant shall deposit the sum of _____________ to be held by the Landlord as security deposit for reasonable repair of damages to, or cleaning of the Premises upon the expiration or termination of this Lease, or other notable damages.

[USE OF PREMISES]

1. Tenant agrees that the Premises shall be used and occupied for no other purpose than as dwelling and that the Premises shall be occupied only by Tenant and the following named adults _____________

____

______________________________ and the following named children ______________

____

__________ and no other without first obtaining a written consent from the Landlord.

2. The tenant hereby agrees to be responsible for the following utilities and or services ___ ___ ___ _

__ ___ ___ ___ ___ ___ ___ ___ ___ ___ ___ ___ ___ ___ ___ _________________

3. The Tenant is responsible for the following maintenance and or repairs ___ ___ ___ ___ ___ __

_ ___ ___ ___ ___ ___ ___ ___ ___ ___ ___ ___ ___ ___ ____ ___ ___ ___

4. The tenant agrees not to keep any pets on the premises without priorly obtaining a written consent from the Landlord.

[ABANDONMENT AND RIGHT TO ENTER]

In any case that the Tenant abandons the Premises during the term of this Agreement, the Landlord has the right to enter the Premises by any means necessary without facing any liability and the Landlord may terminate this Agreement.

[AMENDMENTS]

The Landlord and Tenant agree that any amendments made to this Agreement must be in writing where they must be signed by both the Landlord and the Tenant. As such any amendment made by the parties will be applied to this Agreement.

[GOVERNING LAW]

This Agreement shall be governed by and construed in accordance with the laws of ___ ___ ___ ___

___ ___ ___ ___ ___ ___ ___ ___ ___ ___ ___ ___ ___ ___ ___ _______________

TENANT

Name ___________________________

Signature _________________________

Date ____________________________

Witness __________________________

Phone ___________________________

Address __________________________

____

Signature ________________________

Date ___________________________

LANDLORD

Name __________________________

Signature ________________________

Date __________________________ _

Address _________________________

____

Witness _________________________

Phone __________________________

Address _________________________

Signature___________Date_________

MONTH-TO-MONTH RENTAL AGREEMENT

This lease agreement is made this __________ by and (between/among) _______ ___ ___ ___ ___ ___ ___ [Landlord] and ___ ___ ___ ___ ___ ___, [and other Tenants,] collectively [Tenant]. Each Tenant is jointly and severally liable for the payment of rent to the landlord and performance of all other terms in this Agreement.

[PREMISES]

Landlord hereby leases the premises located at ___ ___ ___ ___ ___ ___ ___ ___ ___ ___

City of ___ ___ ___ ___ ___, State of ___ ___ ___ ___ ___ ___ ___ ___ [Premises] to Tenant.

[LEASE TERM]

The Lease will start on ___ of ___ ___ ___, 20 ___ and will continue as a month-to-month tenancy. To terminate tenancy, the Landlord or Tenant must give the other party a ___ ___ day written notice of lease non-renewal.

[LEASE PAYMENTS]

The Tenant agrees to pay Landlord for the use of the Premises in the amount of $ ___ __, payable in advance on the first day of each month, except when day falls on a legal holiday or weekend, in which case rent is due on the next business day. Rent will be paid to Landlord at Landlord's address provided herein (or to other places as directed by Landlord) by mail to ___ ___ ___ ___ ___ ___ ___ ___ ___ ___ _ __ ___ or in person, at ___ ___ ___ ___ ___ ___ ___ ___ ___ ___ ___ ___ ___ ___ __.

Landlord will accept check made payable to ______________________________________ _or cashier's check made payable to ____ __or payment by ___________________________ to___________________________

[LATE FEE]

Rent paid after the ___ ___ day of each month will be considered as late; and if rent is not paid within ___ ___ days of such due date, Tenant agrees to pay a late fee of ___ ___ ___ per day for every day that the rent is late.

[INSUFFICIENT FUNDS]

Tenant agrees to pay a charge of ___ ___ ___ for each check given by Tenant to Landlord that is returned to landlord for lack of sufficient funds.

[SECURITY DEPOSIT]

Upon execution of this Lease, Tenant shall deposit the sum of _____________to be held by the Landlord as security deposit for reasonable repair of damages to, or cleaning of the Premises upon the expiration or termination of this Lease, or other notable damages.

[USE OF PREMISES]

1. Tenant agrees that the Premises shall be used and occupied for no other purpose than as dwelling and that the Premises shall be occupied only by Tenant and the following named adults _____________

____

______________________________ and the following named children ______________

____

__________ and no other without first obtaining a written consent from the Landlord.

2. The tenant hereby agrees to be responsible for the following utilities and or services ___ ___ ___ _

__ ___ ___ ___ ___ ___ ___ ___ ___ ___ ___ ___ ___ __________________

3. The Tenant is responsible for the following maintenance and or repairs ___ ___ ___ ___ ___ __

_ ___ ___ ___ ___ ___ ___ ___ ___ ___ ___ ___ ___ ___ _____ ___ ___ ___ ___

4. The tenant agrees not to keep any pets on the premises without priorly obtaining a written consent from the Landlord.

[ABANDONMENT AND RIGHT TO ENTER]

In any case that the Tenant abandons the Premises during the term of this Agreement, the Landlord has the right to enter the Premises by any means necessary without facing any liability and the Landlord may terminate this Agreement.

[AMENDMENTS]

The Landlord and Tenant agree that any amendments made to this Agreement must be in writing where they must be signed by both the Landlord and the Tenant. As such any amendment made by the parties will be applied to this Agreement.

[GOVERNING LAW]

This Agreement shall be governed by and construed in accordance with the laws of ___ ___ ___ ___

___ ___ ___ ___ ___ ___ ___ ___ ___ ___ ___ ___ ___ ___ ____________________

TENANT

Name ______________________________

Signature ___________________________

Date _______________________________

Witness _____________________________

Phone ______________________________

Address _____________________________

____

Signature ___________________________

Date ______________________________

LANDLORD

Name ____________________________

Signature __________________________

Date ____________________________ _

Address ___________________________

____

Witness ___________________________

Phone ____________________________

Address ___________________________

Signature___________Date__________

MONTH-TO-MONTH RENTAL AGREEMENT

This lease agreement is made this __________ by and (between/among) _______ ___ ___ ___ ___ ___ ___ [Landlord] and ___ ___ ___ ___ ___ ___, [and other Tenants,] collectively [Tenant]. Each Tenant is jointly and severally liable for the payment of rent to the landlord and performance of all other terms in this Agreement.

[PREMISES]

Landlord hereby leases the premises located at ___ ___ ___ ___ ___ ___ ___ ___ ___ ___ ___ City of ___ ___ ___ ___ ___, State of ___ ___ ___ ___ ___ ___ ___ ___ [Premises] to Tenant.

[LEASE TERM]

The Lease will start on ___ of ___ ___ ___, 20 ___ and will continue as a month-to-month tenancy. To terminate tenancy, the Landlord or Tenant must give the other party a ___ ___ day written notice of lease non-renewal.

[LEASE PAYMENTS]

The Tenant agrees to pay Landlord for the use of the Premises in the amount of $ ___ __, payable in advance on the first day of each month, except when day falls on a legal holiday or weekend, in which case rent is due on the next business day. Rent will be paid to Landlord at Landlord's address provided herein (or to other places as directed by Landlord) by mail to ___ ___ ___ ___ ___ ___ ___ ___ ___ ___ _ __ ___ or in person, at ___ ___ ___ ___ ___ ___ ___ ___ ___ ___ ___ ___ ___ ___ __.
Landlord will accept check made payable to ______________________________________
_or cashier's check made payable to ____
__or payment by ____________________________ to__________________________

[LATE FEE]

Rent paid after the ___ ___ day of each month will be considered as late; and if rent is not paid within ___ ___ days of such due date, Tenant agrees to pay a late fee of ___ ___ ___ per day for every day that the rent is late.

[INSUFFICIENT FUNDS]

Tenant agrees to pay a charge of ___ ___ ___ for each check given by Tenant to Landlord that is returned to landlord for lack of sufficient funds.

[SECURITY DEPOSIT]

Upon execution of this Lease, Tenant shall deposit the sum of _____________to be held by the Landlord as security deposit for reasonable repair of damages to, or cleaning of the Premises upon the expiration or termination of this Lease, or other notable damages.

[USE OF PREMISES]

1. Tenant agrees that the Premises shall be used and occupied for no other purpose than as dwelling and that the Premises shall be occupied only by Tenant and the following named adults _____________

____

_____________________________ and the following named children ______________

____

__________ and no other without first obtaining a written consent from the Landlord.

2. The tenant hereby agrees to be responsible for the following utilities and or services ___ ___ ___ _

__ ___ ___ ___ ___ ___ ___ ___ ___ ___ ___ ___ ___ ___ ________________

3. The Tenant is responsible for the following maintenance and or repairs ___ ___ ___ ___ ___ __

_ ___ ___ ___ ___ ___ ___ ___ ___ ___ ___ ___ ___ ___ _____ ___ ___ ___ ___

4. The tenant agrees not to keep any pets on the premises without priorly obtaining a written consent from the Landlord.

[ABANDONMENT AND RIGHT TO ENTER]

In any case that the Tenant abandons the Premises during the term of this Agreement, the Landlord has the right to enter the Premises by any means necessary without facing any liability and the Landlord may terminate this Agreement.

[AMENDMENTS]

The Landlord and Tenant agree that any amendments made to this Agreement must be in writing where they must be signed by both the Landlord and the Tenant. As such any amendment made by the parties will be applied to this Agreement.

[GOVERNING LAW]

This Agreement shall be governed by and construed in accordance with the laws of ___ ___ ___ ___

___ ___ ___ ___ ___ ___ ___ ___ ___ ___ ___ ___ ___ ___ ____________________

TENANT

Name __________________________

Signature _______________________

Date ___________________________

Witness ________________________

Phone __________________________

Address ________________________

____

Signature _______________________

Date ___________________________

LANDLORD

Name __________________________

Signature _______________________

Date __________________________

Address ________________________

____

Witness ________________________

Phone __________________________

Address ________________________

Signature___________Date_________

MONTH-TO-MONTH RENTAL **AGREEMENT**

This lease agreement is made this __________ by and (between/among) _______ ___ ___ ___ ___ ___ ___ [Landlord] and ___ ___ ___ ___ ___ ___, [and other Tenants,] collectively [Tenant]. Each Tenant is jointly and severally liable for the payment of rent to the landlord and performance of all other terms in this Agreement.

[PREMISES]

Landlord hereby leases the premises located at ___ ___ ___ ___ ___ ___ ___ ___ ___ ___ City of ___ ___ ___ ___ ___, State of ___ ___ ___ ___ ___ ___ ___ [Premises] to Tenant.

[LEASE TERM]

The Lease will start on ___ of ___ ___ ___, 20 ___ and will continue as a month-to-month tenancy. To terminate tenancy, the Landlord or Tenant must give the other party a ___ ___ day written notice of lease non-renewal.

[LEASE PAYMENTS]

The Tenant agrees to pay Landlord for the use of the Premises in the amount of $ ___ __, payable in advance on the first day of each month, except when day falls on a legal holiday or weekend, in which case rent is due on the next business day. Rent will be paid to Landlord at Landlord's address provided herein (or to other places as directed by Landlord) by mail to ___ ___ ___ ___ ___ ___ ___ ___ ___ ___ _ __ ___ or in person, at ___ ___ ___ ___ ___ ___ ___ ___ ___ ___ ___ ___ ___ ___ __.

Landlord will accept check made payable to ___________________________________

_or cashier's check made payable to ______________________________________

__or payment by ___________________________ to___________________________

[LATE FEE]

Rent paid after the ___ ___ day of each month will be considered as late; and if rent is not paid within ___ ___ days of such due date, Tenant agrees to pay a late fee of ___ ___ ___ per day for every day that the rent is late.

[INSUFFICIENT FUNDS]

Tenant agrees to pay a charge of ___ ___ ___ for each check given by Tenant to Landlord that is returned to landlord for lack of sufficient funds.

[SECURITY DEPOSIT]

Upon execution of this Lease, Tenant shall deposit the sum of _____________to be held by the Landlord as security deposit for reasonable repair of damages to, or cleaning of the Premises upon the expiration or termination of this Lease, or other notable damages.

[USE OF PREMISES]

1. Tenant agrees that the Premises shall be used and occupied for no other purpose than as dwelling and that the Premises shall be occupied only by Tenant and the following named adults _____________

____

______________________________ and the following named children _______________

____

__________ and no other without first obtaining a written consent from the Landlord.

2. The tenant hereby agrees to be responsible for the following utilities and or services ___ ___ ___ _

__ ___ ___ ___ ___ ___ ___ ___ ___ ___ ___ ___ ___ ___ _________________

3. The Tenant is responsible for the following maintenance and or repairs ___ ___ ___ ___ ___ __

_ ___ ___ ___ ___ ___ ___ ___ ___ ___ ___ ___ ___ ___ _____ ___ ___ ___ ___

4. The tenant agrees not to keep any pets on the premises without priorly obtaining a written consent from the Landlord.

[ABANDONMENT AND RIGHT TO ENTER]

In any case that the Tenant abandons the Premises during the term of this Agreement, the Landlord has the right to enter the Premises by any means necessary without facing any liability and the Landlord may terminate this Agreement.

[AMENDMENTS]

The Landlord and Tenant agree that any amendments made to this Agreement must be in writing where they must be signed by both the Landlord and the Tenant. As such any amendment made by the parties will be applied to this Agreement.

[GOVERNING LAW]

This Agreement shall be governed by and construed in accordance with the laws of ___ ___ ___ ___

___ ___ ___ ___ ___ ___ ___ ___ ___ ___ ___ ___ ___ ____________________

TENANT

Name ___________________________

Signature ______________________

Date ____________________________

Witness _________________________

Phone __________________________

Address _________________________

____

Signature ______________________

Date ___________________________

LANDLORD

Name _________________________

Signature ______________________

Date __________________________

Address _______________________

____

Witness _______________________

Phone ________________________

Address _______________________

Signature___________Date_________

MONTH-TO-MONTH RENTAL **AGREEMENT**

This lease agreement is made this __________ by and (between/among) ___________________ ___ ___ ___ [Landlord] and ___ ___ ___ ___ ___ ___, [and other Tenants,] collectively [Tenant]. Each Tenant is jointly and severally liable for the payment of rent to the landlord and performance of all other terms in this Agreement.

[PREMISES]

Landlord hereby leases the premises located at ___ ___ ___ ___ ___ ___ ___ ___ ___ ___ City of ___ ___ ___ ___ ___, State of ___ ___ ___ ___ ___ ___ ___ ___ [Premises] to Tenant.

[LEASE TERM]

The Lease will start on ___ of ___ ___ ___, 20 ___ and will continue as a month-to-month tenancy. To terminate tenancy, the Landlord or Tenant must give the other party a ___ ___ day written notice of lease non-renewal.

[LEASE PAYMENTS]

The Tenant agrees to pay Landlord for the use of the Premises in the amount of $ ___ __, payable in advance on the first day of each month, except when day falls on a legal holiday or weekend, in which case rent is due on the next business day. Rent will be paid to Landlord at Landlord's address provided herein (or to other places as directed by Landlord) by mail to ___ ___ ___ ___ ___ ___ ___ ___ ___ ___ _ __ ___ or in person, at ___ ___ ___ ___ ___ ___ ___ ___ ___ ___ ___ ___ ___ ___ __.
Landlord will accept check made payable to ____
_or cashier's check made payable to ____
__or payment by ___________________________to_______________________________

[LATE FEE]

Rent paid after the ___ ___ day of each month will be considered as late; and if rent is not paid within ___ ___ days of such due date, Tenant agrees to pay a late fee of ___ ___ ___ per day for every day that the rent is late.

[INSUFFICIENT FUNDS]

Tenant agrees to pay a charge of ___ ___ ___ for each check given by Tenant to Landlord that is returned to landlord for lack of sufficient funds.

[SECURITY DEPOSIT]

Upon execution of this Lease, Tenant shall deposit the sum of _____________to be held by the Landlord as security deposit for reasonable repair of damages to, or cleaning of the Premises upon the expiration or termination of this Lease, or other notable damages.

[USE OF PREMISES]

1. Tenant agrees that the Premises shall be used and occupied for no other purpose than as dwelling and that the Premises shall be occupied only by Tenant and the following named adults _____________

____

______________________________ and the following named children _______________

____

__________ and no other without first obtaining a written consent from the Landlord.

2. The tenant hereby agrees to be responsible for the following utilities and or services ___ ___ ___ _

__ ___ ___ ___ ___ ___ ___ ___ ___ ___ ___ ___ ___ ___ ___ _________________

3. The Tenant is responsible for the following maintenance and or repairs ___ ___ ___ ___ ___ __

_ ___ ___ ___ ___ ___ ___ ___ ___ ___ ___ ___ ___ ___ _____ ___ ___ ___ ___

4. The tenant agrees not to keep any pets on the premises without priorly obtaining a written consent from the Landlord.

[ABANDONMENT AND RIGHT TO ENTER]

In any case that the Tenant abandons the Premises during the term of this Agreement, the Landlord has the right to enter the Premises by any means necessary without facing any liability and the Landlord may terminate this Agreement.

[AMENDMENTS]

The Landlord and Tenant agree that any amendments made to this Agreement must be in writing where they must be signed by both the Landlord and the Tenant. As such any amendment made by the parties will be applied to this Agreement.

[GOVERNING LAW]

This Agreement shall be governed by and construed in accordance with the laws of ___ ___ ___ ___

___ ___ ___ ___ ___ ___ ___ ___ ___ ___ ___ ___ ___ _____________________

TENANT

Name ______________________________

Signature ___________________________

Date _______________________________

Witness _____________________________

Phone ______________________________

Address _____________________________

____

Signature __________________________

Date _____________________________

LANDLORD

Name ______________________________

Signature ___________________________

Date ____________________________ _

Address _____________________________

____

Witness _____________________________

Phone _______________________________

Address _____________________________

Signature___________Date__________

MONTH-TO-MONTH RENTAL **AGREEMENT**

This lease agreement is made this __________ by and (between/among) _______ ___ ___ ___ ___ ___ ___ [Landlord] and ___ ___ ___ ___ ___ ___, [and other Tenants,] collectively [Tenant]. Each Tenant is jointly and severally liable for the payment of rent to the landlord and performance of all other terms in this Agreement.

[PREMISES]

Landlord hereby leases the premises located at ___ ___ ___ ___ ___ ___ ___ ___ ___ ___ City of ___ ___ ___ ___ ___, State of ___ ___ ___ ___ ___ ___ ___ [Premises] to Tenant.

[LEASE TERM]

The Lease will start on ___ of ___ ___ ___, 20 ___ and will continue as a month-to-month tenancy. To terminate tenancy, the Landlord or Tenant must give the other party a ___ ___ day written notice of lease non-renewal.

[LEASE PAYMENTS]

The Tenant agrees to pay Landlord for the use of the Premises in the amount of $ ___ __, payable in advance on the first day of each month, except when day falls on a legal holiday or weekend, in which case rent is due on the next business day. Rent will be paid to Landlord at Landlord's address provided herein (or to other places as directed by Landlord) by mail to ___ ___ ___ ___ ___ ___ ___ ___ ___ ___ _ __ ___ or in person, at ___ ___ ___ ___ ___ ___ ___ ___ ___ ___ ___ ___ ___ ___.

Landlord will accept check made payable to ______________________________________ _or cashier's check made payable to ____ __or payment by ___________________________ to___________________________

[LATE FEE]

Rent paid after the ___ ___ day of each month will be considered as late; and if rent is not paid within ___ ___ days of such due date, Tenant agrees to pay a late fee of ___ ___ ___ per day for every day that the rent is late.

[INSUFFICIENT FUNDS]

Tenant agrees to pay a charge of ___ ___ ___ for each check given by Tenant to Landlord that is returned to landlord for lack of sufficient funds.

[SECURITY DEPOSIT]

Upon execution of this Lease, Tenant shall deposit the sum of _____________to be held by the Landlord as security deposit for reasonable repair of damages to, or cleaning of the Premises upon the expiration or termination of this Lease, or other notable damages.

[USE OF PREMISES]

1. Tenant agrees that the Premises shall be used and occupied for no other purpose than as dwelling and that the Premises shall be occupied only by Tenant and the following named adults _____________

____

____________________________ and the following named children ______________

____

_________ and no other without first obtaining a written consent from the Landlord.

2. The tenant hereby agrees to be responsible for the following utilities and or services ___ ___ ___ _

__ ___ ___ ___ ___ ___ ___ ___ ___ ___ ___ ___ ___ ___ ________________

3. The Tenant is responsible for the following maintenance and or repairs ___ ___ ___ ___ ___ __

_ ___ ___ ___ ___ ___ ___ ___ ___ ___ ___ ___ ___ ___ _____ ___ ___ ___

4. The tenant agrees not to keep any pets on the premises without priorly obtaining a written consent from the Landlord.

[ABANDONMENT AND RIGHT TO ENTER]

In any case that the Tenant abandons the Premises during the term of this Agreement, the Landlord has the right to enter the Premises by any means necessary without facing any liability and the Landlord may terminate this Agreement.

[AMENDMENTS]

The Landlord and Tenant agree that any amendments made to this Agreement must be in writing where they must be signed by both the Landlord and the Tenant. As such any amendment made by the parties will be applied to this Agreement.

[GOVERNING LAW]

This Agreement shall be governed by and construed in accordance with the laws of ___ ___ ___ ___

___ ___ ___ ___ ___ ___ ___ ___ ___ ___ ___ ___ ___ ___ ___ ___________________

TENANT

Name ____________________________

Signature _________________________

Date _____________________________

Witness ___________________________

Phone ____________________________

Address ___________________________

____

Signature ________________________

Date ____________________________

LANDLORD

Name ___________________________

Signature _________________________

Date ___________________________

Address __________________________

____

Witness __________________________

Phone ____________________________

Address __________________________

Signature___________Date___________

Made in the USA
Middletown, DE
02 August 2024